THE BUILDING
BLOCKS OF LIFE

EXAMINING FUNGI AND PROTISTS

Edited by **Louise Eaton** and **Kara Rogers**

Britannica®
Educational Publishing

IN ASSOCIATION WITH

ROSEN
EDUCATIONAL SERVICES

Published in 2018 by Britannica Educational Publishing (a trademark of Encyclopædia Britannica, Inc.) in association with The Rosen Publishing Group, Inc. 29 East 21st Street, New York, NY 10010

Distributed exclusively by Rosen Publishing.
To see additional Britannica Educational Publishing titles, go to rosenpublishing.com.

Britannica Educational Publishing
J.E. Luebering: Executive Director, Core Editorial
Andrea R. Field: Managing Editor, Compton's by Britannica

Rosen Publishing
Meredith Day: Editor
Nelson Sá: Art Director
Brian Garvey: Series Designer
Ellina Litmanovich: Book Layout
Cindy Reiman: Photography Manager
Nicole DiMella: Photo Researcher

Library of Congress Cataloging-in-Publication Data

Names: Eaton, Louise, editor. | Rogers, Kara, editor.
Title: Examining fungi and protists / edited by Louise Eaton and Kara Rogers.
Description: New York : Britannica Educational Publishing in Association with Rosen Educational Services, 2018. | Series: The building blocks of life | Audience: Grades 9-12. | Includes bibliographical references and index.
Identifiers: LCCN 2017011648 | ISBN 9781538300084 (library bound : alk. paper)
Subjects: LCSH: Fungi--Juvenile literature. | Protista--Juvenile literature.
Classification: LCC QK603.5 .E93 2018 | DDC 579--dc23
LC record available at https://lccn.loc.gov/2017011648

Manufactured in Malaysia

Photo credits: Cover, p. 1 (DNA) Jezperklauzen/iStock/Thinkstock; cover. p. 1 (paramecium) NNehring//E+/Getty Images; p. 12 U.S. Department of Energy/www.flickr.com/photos/departmentofenergy/9525866984/; p. 18 Popperfoto/Getty Images; p. 21 Whiteaster/Shutterstock.com; p. 28 Dr. Philippa Uwins, Whistler Research Pty./Science Source; p. 31 Arterra/Universal Images Group/Getty Images; pp. 39, 136 © AP Images; p. 44 Steve Gschmeissner/Science Source; p. 50 Zamytskiy Leonid/Shutterstock.com; p. 69 mapichai/Shutterstock.com; p. 72 photowind/Shutterstock.com; p. 80 Worraket/Shutterstock.com; p. 86 Olivier Morin/AFP/Getty Images; p. 91 Mirko Graul/ Shutterstock.com; p. 104 Vadym Zaitsev/Shutterstock.com; p. 106 TTphoto/Shutterstock.com; p. 111 Encyclopædia Britannica, Inc.; p. 116 Nancy R. Schiff/Archive Photos/Getty Images; p. 119 Roland Birke/Photolibrary/Getty Images; p. 134 Steve Gschmeissner/Science Photo Library/Getty Images; p. 147 © Merriam-Webster, Inc.; p. 153 Kent Wood/Science Source; p. 165 D. Kucharski K. Kucharska/Shutterstock; p. 173 Gertjan Hooijer/Shutterstock.com; p. 180 Adwo/Shutterstock.com; p. 184 Apexphotos/Moment Open/Getty Images; p. 192 Eo naya/Shutterstock.com; p. 194 David McNew/Getty Images; p. 223 Michael Patrick O'Neill/Science Source/Getty Images; p. 231 FLPA/Robert Canis/SuperStock; p. 237 Shubhashish Chakrabarty/Shutterstock.com; p. 242 Universal Images Group/Getty Images.

CONTENTS

INTRODUCTION 8

CHAPTER 1
FEATURES OF FUNGI AND LICHENS.. 14

IMPORTANCE OF FUNGI... 15

DISCOVERING PENICILLIN 17

SIZE RANGE AND DISTRIBUTION OF FUNGI........................... 20

STRUCTURE OF FUNGI... 22

THE THALLUS 23

SPOROPHORES AND SPORES 27

GROWTH OF FUNGI 29

NUTRITION OF FUNGI 34

SAPROBIOSIS 35

PARASITISM IN PLANTS AND INSECTS........................... 37

PARASITISM IN HUMANS....................................... 42

MYCORRHIZA 45

PREDATION 47

LICHENS.. 48

BASIC FEATURES... 49

FORM AND FUNCTION 53

CHAPTER 2
REPRODUCTION AND ECOLOGY OF FUNGI............................... 61

REPRODUCTIVE PROCESSES....................................... 62

ASEXUAL REPRODUCTION 62

SEXUAL REPRODUCTION....................................... 64

SEXUAL INCOMPATIBILITY..................................... 66

PHEROMONES... 67

Life Cycles 68
Ecology 70
    Research on Fungi Life Cycles 71

CHAPTER 3

TYPES OF FUNGI AND LICHENS 74
  Select Types of Fungi 76
    Ascomycota 76
    Chestnut Blight 78
    Basidiomycota 90
    Microsporidia 101
    Oomycota 102
    Late Blight 103
  Select Types of Lichens 105
    Beard Lichen 105
    Iceland Moss 107
    Oak Moss 107
    Parmelia 108

CHAPTER 4

FEATURES OF PROTISTS 110
  General Features 113
    Research on Eukaryotic Cell Development 115
  Form and Function 117
    Locomotion 118
    Respiration and Nutrition 124
    Reproduction and Life Cycles 127
  Ecology 133
  Evolution and Paleoprotistology 139

CHAPTER 5

TYPES OF PROTOZOANS 145
  Classification Problems 148
  Select Groups of Protozoans 151
    Amoeba 151

CILIATE 153

EUGLENA 155

FLAGELLATE.. 156

FORAMINIFERAN 157

GREGARINE 158

HELIOFLAGELLATE 159

HELIOZOAN 160

LEISHMANIA 161

MYXOMYCETES 162

OPALINID 163

PARAMECIUM 164

PLASMODIUM 167

TREATING AND ERADICATING MALARIA 168

RADIOLARIAN 171

SLIME MOLD 172

STENTOR 174

TRICHOMONAD..175

TRYPANOSOMA...176

VORTICELLA 176

ZOOFLAGELLATE..177

CHAPTER 6

FEATURES OF ALGAE 179

SIZE RANGE AND DISTRIBUTION.............................. 182

ECOLOGICAL IMPORTANCE OF ALGAE 186

COMMERCIAL IMPORTANCE 187

TOXICITY 193

FORM AND FUNCTION 196

ALGAL CELL FEATURES...................................... 196

FLAGELLA 201

MITOSIS 203

CELLULAR RESPIRATION..................................... 203

LIGHT ABSORBTION 204

NUTRIENT STORAGE.. 206

REPRODUCTION AND LIFE CYCLES 208

EVOLUTION AND PALEONTOLOGY 212

CHAPTER 7

TYPES OF ALGAE... 219
    CLASSIFICATION FEATURES 220
    SELECT GROUPS OF ALGAE...................................... 222
        GREEN ALGAE... 222
        BROWN ALGAE 230
        DINOFLAGELLATES 236
        RED TIDE 239
        RED ALGAE 241

CONCLUSION 246
GLOSSARY 247
BIBLIOGRAPHY 250
INDEX 254

INTRODUCTION

Fungi, protists, and algae are extraordinarily diverse organisms that differ fundamentally in their biological and ecological characteristics. Yet they share a common evolutionary history, having arisen within the lineage of eukaryotic life (organisms with a clearly defined nucleus), as opposed to the lineage of prokaryotic life (organisms that lack a distinct nucleus). Thus, fungi and protists are more closely related to animals and plants, which are eukaryotes, than they are to bacteria and the primitive archaea, which are prokaryotes.

Most fungi are readily recognizable in nature, since many members of the group, such as shelf fungi found growing on trees and chanterelles growing up from forest soils, are macroscopic and hence are easily observed with the naked eye. Single-celled yeast, however, can be seen only with the aid of a microscope. Still, they are grouped with the fungi because they possess reproductive structures common to other types of fungi. Some yeast actually produce special filaments known as hyphae, which in yeast are microscopic versions of the structures that give rise to puffballs and umbrella-shaped mushrooms.

All fungi are classified in the kingdom Fungi, which includes the yeasts, rusts, smuts, mildews, molds, mushrooms, and toadstools. There are also many fungus-like organisms, including slime molds and oomycetes, that do not belong to kingdom Fungi but are often called fungi. Many of these fungus-like organisms are included in the kingdom Chromista. Fungi are among the most widely distributed organisms on Earth and are of great environmental and medical importance. Many fungi are free-living, in soil or water. Other species form parasitic or symbiotic relationships with plants or animals.

Historically, the fungi were included in the plant kingdom. However, because fungi lack chlorophyll and are distinguished by unique structural and physiological features (i.e., components of the cell wall and cell membrane), they have been separated from plants. In addition, the fungi are clearly distinguished from all other living organisms, including animals, by their principal modes of vegetative growth and nutrient intake. Fungi grow from the tips of filaments (hyphae) that make up the bodies of the organisms (mycelia), and they digest organic matter externally before absorbing it into their mycelia. While mushrooms and toadstools (poisonous mushrooms) are by no means the most numerous or economically significant fungi, they are the most easily recognized fungi. The Latin word for mushroom, *fungus* (plural *fungi*), has come to stand for the whole group. Similarly, the study of fungi is known as mycology—a broad application of the Greek word for mushroom, *mykēs*. Fungi other than mushrooms are sometimes collectively called molds, although this term is better restricted to fungi of the sort represented by bread mold.

Many protists are single-celled "animals," and thus their relationship to other single-celled organisms, including yeast and bacteria, as well as to creatures in the animal kingdom, was long a source of confusion. Today, however, scientists know that protists are as different from one another as they are from all other life on Earth. For this reason, they are often described ambiguously as organisms other than fungi, plants, and animals. Thousands of species of protists exist, and scientists believe that just as many if not more are still undiscovered.

Protists are commonly divided into three categories. Protozoans (which comes from the Greek words *protos*, meaning "first," and *zoions*, meaning "animals") are generally heterotrophic, meaning that they obtain food from other organisms. The plantlike algae are autotrophic, meaning that they can make their own food through the process of photosynthesis. The funguslike slime molds and water molds are usually saprotrophic, meaning that they feed on decaying matter.

Protists are distributed throughout the world. Many live in the oceans or in freshwater, where they may be either bottom-dwellers or free floaters. Other protists live on land and can be found in soils, forest litter, desert sands, and on the bark and leaves of trees. Cysts and spores may be recovered from considerable heights in the atmosphere, and some researchers claim that certain algal protists actually live, and perhaps reproduce, in air streams. In addition, some protists are parasites and live on or within the bodies of plants and animals.

Protists may live as solitary individuals or in groups called colonies. Although many protists are microscopic and commonly range from 5 micrometers (0.002 inch) to 2 or 3 millimeters (0.07 or 0.1 inch), a number of algae species are macroscopic and can reach several meters in length. While the vast majority of protozoans move by means of flagella ("whips") or cilia (small "hairs"), algae are commonly non-motile or free-floating.

A number of protists cause serious diseases. For example, the protist *Trypanosoma* causes the

Scientists at the National Renewable Energy Laboratory are studying algae to see if it can be used as a source of biofuels. This reactor uses light energy to stimulate photosynthesis and grow algae.

disease African sleeping sickness in humans, while a particular species of amoeba is responsible for a form of dysentery.

Algae are a diverse group of organisms, ranging from those that appear as a green stain on damp rocks and tree trunks to those that form a fine scum on quiet ponds and the massive seaweeds that float in the ocean. In general, algae are organisms that are made up of one or more eukaryotic cells (cells with a true nucleus) that contain chlorophyll and that are less complex than plants. Many types of algae consist of single cells. Other types are colonial or can form filaments of cells. Some, such as kelp, have simple tissues. Many thousands of marine and freshwater species of algae have been described. Dense growth of algae, called blooms, may discolour the water, deplete its oxygen content, poison aquatic animals and waterfowl, and irritate the skin and respiratory tract of humans.

The fascinating world of fungi, protists, and algae has been a source of scientific intrigue for centuries. These organisms individually and collectively have vital roles in nature and in human societies, serving as sources of food and medicines and as resources for the development of new biotechnologies. They also represent some of Earth's most evolutionarily mysterious life forms, and hence it is no wonder that fungi, protists, and algae are the subjects of research in a wide variety of scientific fields.

FEATURES OF FUNGI AND LICHENS

Scientists estimate there are probably 1.5 million species of fungi worldwide, though only about 99,000 species have been described. These species share similar structural elements and other features despite their variety in appearance. Another type of organism related to fungi is the lichen. Each lichen is formed of one or two species of fungi and an alga or cyanobacteria living together so intimately as to seem like a single, plantlike organism. The lichens are one of the best illustrations of symbiosis, the intimate living together of two or three different kinds of organisms. There are about 15,000 different kinds of lichens distributed worldwide. They are especially suited for growth in harsh regions, where few plants can survive.

IMPORTANCE OF FUNGI

Humans have been indirectly aware of fungi since the first loaf of leavened bread was baked and the first tub of grape must was turned into wine. Ancient peoples were familiar with the ravages of fungi in agriculture but attributed these diseases to the wrath of the gods. The Romans designated a particular deity, Robigus, as the god of the rust disease and, in an effort to appease him, organized an annual festival, the Robigalia, in his honour.

Fungi are everywhere in very large numbers—in the soil and the air, in lakes, rivers, and seas, on and within plants and animals, in food and clothing, and in the human body. Together with bacteria, fungi are responsible for breaking down organic matter and releasing carbon, oxygen, nitrogen, and phosphorus into the soil and the atmosphere. Fungi are essential to many household and industrial processes, notably the making of bread, wine, beer, and certain cheeses. Fungi are also used as food; for example, some mushrooms, morels, and truffles are epicurean delicacies, and mycoproteins (fungal proteins), derived from the mycelia of certain species of fungi, are used to make foods that are high in protein.

Mycology, or the study of fungi, has greatly contributed to the accumulation of fundamental knowledge in biology. For example, studies of ordinary baker's or brewer's yeast (*Saccharomyces cerevisiae*) led to discoveries of basic cellular biochemistry and metabolism. Some of these pioneering discoveries were made at the end of the 19th century and continued during the first half of the 20th century. From 1920 through the 1940s, geneticists and biochemists who studied mutants of the red bread mold, *Neurospora*, established the one-gene–one-enzyme theory, thus contributing to the foundation of modern genetics. Fungi continue to be useful for studying cell and molecular biology, genetic engineering, and other basic disciplines of biology.

The medical relevance of fungi was discovered in 1928, when Scottish bacteriologist Alexander Fleming noticed the green mold *Penicillum notatum* growing in a culture dish of *Staphylococcus* bacteria. Around the spot of mold was a clear ring in which no bacteria grew. Fleming successfully isolated the substance from the mold that inhibited the growth of bacteria. In 1929 he published a scientific report announcing the discovery of penicillin, the first of a series of antibiotics—many of them derived from fungi—that have revolutionized medical practice.

Another medically important fungus is *Claviceps purpurea*, which is commonly called ergot and causes a plant disease of the same name. The disease is characterized by a growth that develops on grasses, especially on rye. Ergot is a source of several chemicals used in drugs that induce labour in pregnant women and that control hemorrhage after

DISCOVERING PENICILLIN

Scottish bacteriologist Sir Alexander Fleming (1881–1955), Australian pathologist Howard Walter Florey and British biochemist Ernst Boris Chain received the Nobel Prize for Physiology or Medicine in 1945 for their work with penicillin.

Fleming had a genius for technical ingenuity and original observation. His work on wound infection and lysozyme, an antibacterial enzyme found in tears and saliva, guaranteed him a place in the history of bacteriology. But it was his discovery of penicillin in 1928 which started the antibiotic revolution, that sealed his lasting reputation.

On Sept. 3, 1928, shortly after his appointment as professor of bacteriology, Fleming noticed that a culture plate of *Staphylococcus aureus* he had been working on had become contaminated by a fungus. A mold, later identified as *Penicllium notatum* (also called *P. chrysogenum*), had inhibited the growth of the bacteria. He at first called the substance "mould juice" and then "penicillin," after the mold that produces it. Fleming decided to investigate further, because he thought that he had found an enzyme more potent than lysozyme. In fact, it was not an enzyme but an antibiotic—one of the first to be discovered. By the time Fleming had established this, he was interested in penicillin for itself. Very much the lone researcher with an eye for the unusual, Fleming had the freedom to pursue anything that interested him. While this

(continued on page 19)

Alexander Fleming, seen here at work in 1943, discovered penicillin, an antibiotic agent that can treat many different kinds of infections.

(continued from page 17)

approach was ideal for taking advantage of a chance observation, the therapeutic development of penicillin required multidisciplinary teamwork. Fleming, working with two young researchers, failed to stabilize and purify penicillin. However, he did point out that penicillin had clinical potential, both as a topical antiseptic and as an injectable antibiotic, if it could be isolated and purified.

Later, Florey and Chain isolated and purified penicillin for general clinical use and developed methods for its production. Following World War II and the work of Florey's research team in North Africa, penicillin came into widespread clinical use. Though Florey, Chain, and Fleming shared the 1945 Nobel Prize, their relationship was clouded due to the issue of who should gain the most credit for penicillin. Fleming's role was emphasized by the press because of the romance of his chance discovery and his greater willingness to speak to journalists.

birth. Ergot is also the source of lysergic acid, the active principle of the psychedelic drug lysergic acid diethylamide (LSD). Other species of fungi contain chemicals that are extracted and used to produce drugs known as statins, which control cholesterol levels and ward off coronary heart disease. Fungi are also used in the production of a number of organic acids, enzymes, and vitamins. They have important applications in the dairy, wine, and baking industries and in the production of dyes and inks.

Fungi come in a variety of shapes and sizes and are able to obtain nutrients in different ways. The morphology, or form, of each different type of fungus is related to the mechanisms it uses for growth and reproduction. In addition, the types of metabolic enzymes a fungus synthesizes determine which substances it can break down and utilize for nutrients.

To grow, all fungi require a source of carbon and a source of energy, which can be obtained in any of a variety of ways. For example, whereas some fungi utilize sugars or starches found in organic matter, others obtain nourishment through symbiotic or parasitic relationships with plant or animal hosts. Fungi are characterized by both the metabolic processes they employ as well as by the type of relationship they have with their environment or host.

SIZE RANGE AND DISTRIBUTION OF FUNGI

Because of their size, mushrooms are easily seen in fields and forests and were the only fungi known before microscopes became more common in the 17th century. The microscope made it possible to recognize and identify the great variety of fungal species living on dead or living organic matter. The part of a fungus that is generally visible is the fruiting body, or sporophore. Sporophores vary greatly in size, shape, colour, and longevity. Some are microscopic and completely invisible to the unaided eye; others are no larger than a pin head; still others are gigantic structures. Among the largest sporophores are those of mushrooms, bracket fungi, and puffballs. Some mushrooms reach a diameter of 20 to 25 cm (8 to 10 inches) and a height of 25 to 30 cm (10 to 12

Ganoderma, also referred to as bracket fungi, grow on trees in groups of horizontal rows.

inches). Bracket fungi can reach 40 cm (16 inches) or more in diameter, and puffballs often exceed that size. The largest puffballs on record measured 150 cm (5 feet) in diameter. The number of spores within such giants reaches several trillion.

Fungi are either terrestrial or aquatic, the latter living in freshwater or marine environments. Freshwater species are usually found in clean, cool water because they do not tolerate high degrees of salinity. However, some species are found in slightly brackish water, and a few thrive in highly polluted streams. On land, fungi are found in all temperate and tropical regions of the world where there is sufficient moisture to enable them to grow. Soil that is rich in organic matter furnishes an ideal habitat for a large number of species. In contrast, only a small number of species are found in drier areas or in habitats with little or no organic matter. A few species of fungi live in the Arctic and Antarctic regions, although they are rare and are more often found living in symbiosis with algae in the form of lichens. Mycologists estimate that there may be as many as 1.5 million total species of fungi on Earth, though only about 99,000 species have been identified and described.

STRUCTURE OF FUNGI

A typical fungus consists of a mass of branched, tubular filaments enclosed by a rigid cell wall. The filaments, called hyphae (singular hypha), branch repeatedly into a complicated, radially expanding network called the mycelium, which makes up the thallus, or undifferentiated body, of the typical fungus. The mycelium grows by utilizing nutrients from the environment and, upon reaching a certain stage of maturity, forms—either directly or in special fruiting bodies—reproductive cells called spores. The spores are released and dispersed by a wide variety of passive or active mechanisms; upon reaching a suitable substrate, the spores germinate and develop hyphae that grow, branch repeatedly, and become the mycelium of the new individual. Fungal growth is mainly confined to the tips of the hyphae, and all fungal structures are therefore made up of hyphae or portions of hyphae.

Some fungi, notably the yeasts, do not form a mycelium but grow as individual cells that multiply by budding or, in certain species, by fission.

THE THALLUS

In almost all fungi the hyphae that make up the thallus have cell walls. (The thalli of the true slime molds lack cell walls and, for this and other reasons, are classified as protists rather than fungi.) A hypha is a multibranched tubular cell filled with cytoplasm. The tube itself may be either continuous throughout or divided into compartments, or cells, by cross walls called septa (singular septum). In nonseptate (i.e., coenocytic) hyphae the nuclei are scattered throughout the cytoplasm. In septate hyphae each cell may contain one to many nuclei, depending on the type of fungus or the stage of hyphal development. The cells of fungi are similar in structure to those of many other organisms. The minute nucleus, readily seen only in young portions of the hypha, is surrounded by a double membrane and typically contains one nucleolus. In addition to the nucleus, various organelles—such as the endoplasmic reticulum, Golgi apparatus, ribosomes, and liposomes—are scattered throughout the cytoplasm.

Hyphae usually are either nonseptate (generally in the more primitive fungi) or incompletely septate (meaning that the septa are perforated). This permits the movement of cytoplasm (cytoplasmic streaming) from one cell to the next. In fungi with perforated septa, various molecules are able to move rapidly between hyphal cells, but the movement of larger organelles, such as mitochondria and nuclei, is prevented. In the absence of septa, both mitochondria and nuclei can be readily translocated along hyphae. In mating interactions between filamentous Basidiomycota, the nuclei of one parent often invade the hyphae of the other parent, because the septa are degraded ahead of the incoming nuclei to allow their passage through the existing hyphae. Once the incoming nuclei are established, septa are re-formed.

Variations in the structure of septa are numerous in the fungi. Some fungi have sieve-like septa called pseudosepta, whereas fungi in other groups have septa with one to few pores that are small enough in size to prevent the movement of nuclei to adjacent cells. Basidiomycota have a septal structure called a dolipore septum that is composed of a pore cap surrounding a septal swelling and septal pore. This organization permits cytoplasm and small organelles to pass through but restricts the movement of nuclei to varying degrees.

The wall of the hypha is complex in both composition and structure. Its exact chemical composition varies in different fungal groups. In some fungus-like organisms the wall contains considerable quantities of cellulose, a complex carbohydrate that is the chief constituent of the cell walls of plants. two other polymers—chitin and glucan—form the main structural components of the wall. Some chemical substances in the walls of fungi serve to thicken or toughen the wall, thus imparting rigidity and strength. The chemical composition of the wall of a particular fungus may vary at different stages of the organism's growth—a possible indication that the wall plays some part in determining the form of the fungus. In some fungi, carbohydrates are stored in the wall at one stage of development and are removed and utilized at a later stage. In some yeasts, fusion of sexually functioning cells is brought about by the interaction of specific chemical substances on the walls of two compatible mating types.

When the mycelium grows in or on a surface, such as in the soil, on a log, or in a culture medium, it appears as a mass of loose, cottony threads. The richer the composition of the growth medium, the more profuse the threads and the more feltlike the mass. On the sugar-rich growth substances used in laboratories, the assimilative (somatic) hyphae are so interwoven as to form a thick, almost leathery colony. On the soil, inside a leaf, in the skin of animals, or in other parasitized plant or animal tissues, the hyphae are usually spread in a loose network. The mycelia of the so-called higher fungi does, however, become organized at times into compact masses of different sizes that serve various functions. Some of these masses, called sclerotia, become extremely hard and serve to carry the fungus over periods of adverse conditions of temperature and moisture. One example of a fungus that forms sclerotia is *Claviceps purpurea*, which causes ergot, a disease of cereal grasses such as rye. The underground sclerotia of *Poria cocos*, an edible pore fungus also known as tuckahoe, may reach a diameter of 20 to 25 cm (8 to 10 inches).

Various other tissues are also produced by the interweaving of the assimilative hyphae of some fungi. Stromata (singular stroma) are cushion-like tissues that bear spores in various ways. Rhizomorphs are long strands of parallel hyphae cemented together. Those of the honey mushroom (*Armillaria mellea*), which are black and resemble shoestrings, are intricately constructed and are differentiated to conduct water and food materials from one part of the thallus to another.

SPOROPHORES AND SPORES

When the mycelium of a fungus reaches a certain stage of growth, it begins to produce spores either directly on the somatic hyphae or, more often, on special sporiferous (spore-produced) hyphae, which may be loosely arranged or grouped into intricate structures called fruiting bodies, or sporophores. The more primitive fungi produce spores in sporangia, which are saclike sporophores whose entire cytoplasmic contents cleave into spores, called sporangiospores. Thus, they differ from more advanced fungi in that their asexual spores are endogenous. Sporangiospores are either naked and flagellated (zoospores) or walled and nonmotile (aplanospores). The more primitive aquatic and terrestrial fungi tend to produce zoospores. The zoospores of aquatic fungi and fungus-like organisms swim in the surrounding water by means of one or two variously located flagella (whiplike organs of locomotion). Zoospores produced by terrestrial fungi are released after a rain from the sporangia in which they are borne and swim

Fungal spores, seen here in a colorized scanning electron micrograph, can take many different forms depending on the type of fungus.

for a time in the rainwater between soil particles or on the wet surfaces of plants, where the sporangia are formed by parasitic fungi. After some time, the zoospores lose their flagella, surround themselves with walls, and encyst. Each cyst germinates by producing a germ tube.

The germ tube may develop a mycelium or a reproductive structure, depending on the species and on the environmental conditions. The bread molds, which are the most advanced of the primitive fungi, produce only aplanospores (nonmotile spores) in their sporangia.

The more advanced fungi do not produce motile spores of any kind, even though some of them are aquatic in fresh or marine waters. In these fungi, asexually produced spores (usually called conidia) are produced exogenously and are typically formed terminally or laterally on special spore-produced hyphae called conidiophores. Conidiophores may be arranged singly on the hyphae or may be grouped in special asexual fruiting bodies, such as flask-shaped pycnidia, mattress-like acervuli, cushion-shaped sporodochia, or sheaflike synnemata.

GROWTH OF FUNGI

Under favourable environmental conditions, fungal spores germinate and form hyphae. During this process, the spore absorbs water through its wall, the cytoplasm becomes activated, nuclear division takes place, and more cytoplasm is synthesized. The wall initially grows as a spherical structure. Once polarity is established, a hyphal apex forms, and from the wall of the spore a germ tube bulges out, enveloped by a wall of its own that is formed as the germ tube grows.

The hypha may be roughly divided into three regions: (1) the apical zone about 5–10 micrometres (0.0002–0.0004 inch) in length, (2) the subapical region, extending about 40 micrometres back of the apical zone, which is rich in cytoplasmic components, such as nuclei, Golgi apparatus, ribosomes, mitochondria, the endoplasmic reticulum, and vesicles, but is devoid of vacuoles, and (3) the zone of vacuolation, which is characterized by the presence of many vacuoles and the accumulation of lipids.

Growth of hyphae in most fungi takes place almost exclusively in the apical zone (i.e., at the very tip). This is the region where the cell wall extends continuously to produce a long hyphal tube. The cytoplasm within the apical zone is filled with numerous vesicles. These bubble-like structures are usually too small to be seen with an ordinary microscope but are clearly evident under the electron microscope. In higher fungi the apical vesicles can be detected with an ordinary microscope equipped with phase-contrast optics as a round spot with a somewhat diffuse boundary. This body is universally

Mycelium is visible extending from the bottom of the stem of this mushroom (*Baeospora myosura*).

known by its German name, the *Spitzenkörper*, and its position determines the direction of growth of a hypha.

The growing tip eventually gives rise to a branch. This is the beginning of the branched mycelium. Growing tips that come in contact with neighbouring hyphae often fuse with them to form a hyphal net. In such a vigorously growing system, the cytoplasm is in constant motion, streaming toward the growing tips. Eventually, the older hyphae become highly vacuolated and may be stripped of most of their cytoplasm. All living portions of a thallus are potentially capable of growth. If a small piece of mycelium is placed under conditions favourable for growth, it develops into a new thallus, even if no growing tips are included in the severed portion. Growth of a septate mycelium (i.e., with cross walls between adjacent cells) entails the formation of new septa in the young hyphae. Septa are formed by ringlike growth from the wall of the hypha toward the centre until the septa are complete. In the higher fungi the septum stops growing before it is complete; the result is a central pore through which the cytoplasm flows, thus establishing organic connection throughout the thallus. In contrast to plants, in which the position of the septum separating two daughter cells determines the formation of tissues, the fungal septum is always formed at right angles to the axis of growth. As a result, in fungal tissue formation, the creation of parallel hyphae cannot result from longitudinal septum formation but only from outgrowth of a new branch. In fungi, therefore, the mechanism that determines the point of origin and subsequent direction of growth of hyphal branches is the determining factor in developmental morphogenesis. The individual fungus is potentially immortal, because it continues to grow at the hyphal tips as long as conditions remain favourable. It is possible that, in undisturbed places, mycelia exist that have grown continuously for many thousands of years. The older parts of the hyphae die and decompose, releasing nitrogen and other nutrients into the soil.

Some species of endophytic fungi, such as *Neotyphodium* and *Epichloë*, which invade the seeds of grasses (e.g., ryegrass and fescue) and grow within the plant, grow not through extension of the hyphal tips but by intercalary growth, in which the hyphae attach to the growing cells of the plant. This type of growth enables the hyphae of the fungus to grow at the same rate that the plant grows. Intercalary growth of endophytic fungi was discovered in 2007, although for many years scientists suspected that these fungi possessed unique adaptations that allow them to grow as if they were natural parts of their hosts.

The underground network of mushroom hyphae can grow and spread over a very large area, often several metres (yards) in diameter. The underground hyphae obtain food from organic matter in the substratum and grow outward. The hyphal branches at the edge of the mycelium become organized at intervals into elaborate tissues that develop aboveground into mushrooms. Such a circle of mushrooms is known as a fairy ring, because in the Middle Ages it was believed to represent the path of dancing fairies. The ring marks the periphery of an enormous fungus colony, which, if undisturbed, continues to produce ever wider fairy rings year after year. Fungi can grow into enormous colonies. Some thalli of *Armillaria* species, which are pathogens of forest trees, are among the largest and oldest organisms on Earth.

NUTRITION OF FUNGI

Unlike plants, which use carbon dioxide and light as sources of carbon and energy, respectively, fungi meet these two requirements by assimilating pre-formed organic matter. In general, carbohydrates are the preferred carbon source. Fungi can readily absorb and metabolize a variety of soluble carbohydrates, such as glucose, xylose, sucrose, and fructose. Fungi are also characteristically well equipped to use insoluble carbohydrates such as starches, cellulose, and hemicelluloses, as well as very complex hydrocarbons such as lignin. Many fungi can also use proteins as a source of carbon and nitrogen. To use insoluble carbohydrates and proteins, fungi must first digest these polymers extracellularly. Saprotrophic fungi obtain their food from dead organic material; parasitic fungi do so by feeding on living organisms (usually plants), thus causing disease.

Fungi secure food through the action of enzymes (biological catalysts) secreted into the surface on which they are growing; the enzymes digest the food, which then is absorbed directly through the hyphal walls. Food must be in solution in order to enter the hyphae, and the entire mycelial surface of a fungus is capable of absorbing materials dissolved in water.

The rotting of fruits, such as peaches and citrus fruits in storage, demonstrates this phenomenon, in which the infected parts are softened by the action of the fungal enzymes. In brown rot of peaches, the softened area is somewhat larger than the actual area invaded by the hyphae: the periphery of the brown spot has been softened by enzymes that act ahead of the invading mycelium. Cheeses such as Brie and Camembert are matured by enzymes produced by the fungus *Penicillium camemberti*, which grows on the outer surface of some cheeses. Some fungi produce special rootlike hyphae, called rhizoids, which anchor the thallus to the growth surface and probably also absorb food. Many parasitic fungi are even more specialized in this respect, producing special absorptive organs called haustoria.

SAPROBIOSIS

Together with bacteria, saprotrophic fungi are largely responsible for the decomposition of organic matter, including foodstuffs. Certain saprotrophic fungi destroy timber and timber products as their mycelia invade and digest the wood; many of these fungi produce their spores in large, woody, fruiting bodies—e.g., bracket or shelf fungi. Paper, textiles, and leather are often attacked and destroyed by fungi. This is particularly true in tropical regions, where temperature and humidity are often very high.

The nutritional requirements of saprotrophs (and of some parasites that can be cultivated artificially) have been determined by growing fungi experimentally on various synthetic substances of known chemical composition. Fungi usually exhibit the same morphological characteristics in these culture media as they do in nature. Carbon is supplied in the form of sugars or starch. The majority of fungi thrive on such sugars as glucose, fructose, mannose, maltose, and, to a lesser extent, sucrose. Decomposition products of proteins, such as proteoses, peptones, and amino acids, can be used by most fungi as nitrogen sources; ammonium compounds and nitrates also serve as nutrients for many species. It is doubtful, however, that any fungus can combine, or fix, atmospheric nitrogen into usable compounds. Chemical elements such as phosphorus, sulfur, potassium, magnesium, and small quantities of iron, zinc, manganese, and copper are needed by most fungi for vigorous growth. Elements such as calcium, molybdenum, and gallium are required by at least some species. Oxygen and hydrogen are absolute requirements and are supplied in the form of water or are obtained from carbohydrates. Many fungi, deficient in thiamine and biotin, must obtain these vitamins from the environment. Most fungi appear able to synthesize all other vitamins necessary for their growth and reproduction.

As a rule, most fungi are aerobic organisms, meaning they require free oxygen in order to live. Fermentations, however, take place under anaerobic conditions. Knowledge of the physiology of saprotrophic fungi has enabled industry to use several species for fermentation purposes. One of the most important groups of strictly anaerobic fungi are members of the genera *Neocallimastix* (phylum Neocallimastigomycota), which form a crucial component of the microbial population of the rumen of herbivorous mammals. These fungi are able to degrade plant cell wall components, such as cellulose and xylans, that the animals cannot otherwise digest.

PARASITISM IN PLANTS AND INSECTS

In contrast with the saprotrophic fungi, parasitic fungi attack living organisms, penetrate their outer defenses, invade them, and obtain nourishment from living cytoplasm, thereby causing disease and sometimes death of the host. Most pathogenic (disease-causing) fungi are parasites of plants. Most parasites enter the host through a natural opening, such as a stoma (microscopic air pore) in a leaf, a lenticel (small opening through bark) in a stem, a broken plant hair or a hair socket in a fruit, or a wound in the plant. Among the most common and widespread diseases of plants caused by fungi are the various downy mildews (e.g., of grape, onion, tobacco), the powdery mildews (e.g., of grape, cherry, apple, peach, rose, lilac), the smuts (e.g., of corn, wheat, onion), the rusts (e.g., of wheat, oats, beans, asparagus, snapdragon, hollyhock), apple scab, brown rot of stone fruits, and various leaf spots, blights, and wilts. These diseases cause great damage annually throughout the world, destroying many crops and other sources of food. For example, nearly all the chestnut forests of the United States have been destroyed by the chestnut blight fungus, *Cryphonectria parasitica* (formerly known as *Endothia parasitica*), and the elms in both the United States and Europe have been devastated by *Ophiostoma ulmi* (also called *Ceratocystis ulmi*), the fungus that causes Dutch elm disease.

Infection of a plant takes place when the spores of a pathogenic fungus fall on the leaves or the stem of a susceptible host and germinate, each spore producing a germ tube. The tube grows on the surface of the host until it finds an opening; then the tube enters the host, puts out branches between the cells of the host, and forms a mycelial network within the invaded tissue. The germ tubes of some fungi produce special pressing organs called appressoria, from which a microscopic, needlelike peg presses against and punctures the epidermis of the host; after penetration, a mycelium develops in the usual manner. Many parasitic fungi absorb food from the host cells through the hyphal walls appressed

This American chestnut tree (*Castanea dentata*), one of few remaining in the United States, is suffering from blight (*Cryphonectria parasitica*).

against the cell walls of the host's internal tissues. Others produce haustoria (special absorbing structures) that branch off from the intercellular hyphae and penetrate the cells themselves. Haustoria, which may be short, bulbous protrusions or large branched systems filling the whole cell, are characteristically produced by obligate (i.e., invariably parasitic) parasites; some facultative (i.e., occasionally parasitic) parasites such as the potato blight, *Phytophthora infestans*, also produce them. Obligate parasites, which require living cytoplasm and have extremely specialized nutritional requirements, are exceptionally difficult, and often impossible, to grow in a culture dish in a laboratory. Examples of obligate parasites are the downy mildews, the powdery mildews, and the rusts.

Certain fungi form highly specialized parasitic relationships with insects. For example, the fungal genus *Septobasidium* is parasitic on scale insects (order Homoptera) that feed on trees. The mycelium forms elaborate structures over colonies of insects feeding on the bark. Each insect sinks its proboscis (tubular sucking organ) into the bark and remains there the rest of its life, sucking sap. The fungus sinks haustoria into the bodies of some of the insects and feeds on them without killing them. The parasitized insects are, however, rendered sterile.

The perpetuation of the insect species and the

spread of the fungus are accomplished by the unin-
fected members of the colony, which live in fungal
"houses," safe from enemies. Newly hatched scale
insects crawl over the surface of the fungus, which is
at that time sporulating. Fungal spores adhere to the
young insects and germinate. As the young insects
settle down in a new place on the bark to begin
feeding, they establish new fungal colonies. Thus,
part of the insect colony is sacrificed to the fungus
as food in return for the fungal protection provided
for the rest of the insects. The insect is parasitic on
the tree and the fungus is parasitic on the insect, but
the tree is the ultimate victim.

The sooty molds constitute another interesting
ecological group of fungi that are associated with
insects. The majority of sooty molds are tropical or
subtropical, but some species occur in the temperate
zones. All sooty molds are epiphytic (i.e., they grow
on the surfaces of other plants), but only in areas
where scale insects are present. The fungi parasitize
neither the plants nor the insects but rather obtain
their nourishment exclusively from the honeydew
secretions of the scale insects. Growth of the dark
mycelium over the plant leaves, however, is often so
dense as to significantly reduce the intensity of the
light that reaches the leaf surface; this reduction in
turn significantly reduces the rate of photosynthesis. Insect-fungus associations found in the tropical

forests of Central and South America include the unique relationship of leafcutter ants (sometimes called parasol ants) with fungi in the family Lepiotaceae (phylum Basidiomycota). The ants cultivate the fungi in their nests as an ongoing food supply and secrete enzymes that stimulate or suppress the growth of the fungi.

PARASITISM IN HUMANS

Many pathogenic fungi are known to cause diseases of humans and other animals. In humans, parasitic fungi most commonly enter the body through a wound in the epidermis (skin). Such wounds may be insect punctures or accidentally inflicted scratches, cuts, or bruises. One example of a fungus that causes disease in humans is *Claviceps purpurea*, the cause of ergotism (also known as St. Anthony's fire), a disease that was prevalent in northern Europe in the Middle Ages, particularly in regions of high rye-bread consumption. The wind carries the fungal spores of ergot to the flowers of the rye, where the spores germinate, infect and destroy the ovaries of the plant, and replace them with masses of microscopic threads cemented together into a hard fungal structure shaped like a rye kernel but considerably larger and darker. This structure, called an ergot, contains a number of poisonous organic compounds called alkaloids. A mature head of rye may carry several ergots in addition to noninfected kernels. When the grain is harvested, much of the ergot falls to the ground, but some remains on the plants and is mixed with the grain. Although modern grain-cleaning and milling methods have practically eliminated the disease, the contaminated flour may end up in bread and other food products if the ergot is not removed before milling. In addition, the ergot that falls to the ground may be consumed by cattle turned out to graze in rye fields after harvest. Cattle that consume enough ergot may suffer abortion of fetuses or death. In the spring, when the rye is in bloom, the ergot remaining on the ground produces tiny, black, mushroom-shaped bodies that expel large numbers of spores, thus starting a new series of infections.

Other human diseases caused by fungi include athlete's foot, ringworm, aspergillosis, histoplasmosis, and coccidioidomycosis. The yeast *Candida albicans*, a normal inhabitant of the human mouth, throat, colon, and reproductive organs, does not cause disease when it is in ecological balance with other microbes of the digestive system. However, disease, age, and hormonal changes can cause *C. albicans* to grow in a manner that cannot be controlled by the body's defense systems, resulting in candidiasis (called thrush when affecting the mouth). Candidiasis is characterized by symptoms ranging from irritating inflamed patches on the skin or raised

The fungus that causes athlete's foot, *Tinea pedis*, is seen on a human foot in this scanning electron micrograph.

white patches on the tongue to life-threatening invasive infection that damages the lining of the heart or brain. Improved diagnosis and increased international travel, the latter of which has facilitated the spread of tropical pathogenic fungi, have resulted in an increased incidence of fungal disease in humans. In addition, drug therapies used to manage the immune system in transplant and cancer patients weaken the body's defenses against fungal pathogens. Patients infected with human immunodeficiency virus (HIV), the causative agent of acquired immunodeficiency syndrome (AIDS), have similarly weakened immune defenses against fungi, and many AIDS-related deaths are caused by fungal infections (especially infection with *Aspergillus fumigatus*).

MYCORRHIZA

Among symbiotic fungi, those that enter into mycorrhizal relationships and those that enter into relationships with algae to form lichens are probably the best-known. A large number of fungi infect the roots of plants by forming an association with plants called mycorrhiza (plural mycorrhizas or mycorrhizae). This association differs markedly from ordinary root infection, which is responsible for root rot diseases. Mycorrhizal fungi form a non-disease-producing association in which the fungus invades the root to absorb nutrients. Such fungi establish a mutualistic relationship with their host plants, meaning both the plant and the fungus benefit from the association. About 90 percent of land plants have mycorrhizal fungi, especially for mineral nutrients (i.e., phosphorus), and in return the fungus receives nutrients formed by the plant. During winter, when day length is shortened and exposure to sunlight is reduced, some plants produce few or no nutrients and thus depend on fungi for sugars, nitrogenous compounds, and other nutrients that the fungi are able to absorb from waste materials in the soil. By sharing the products it absorbs from the soil with its plant host, a fungus can keep its host alive. In some lowland forests, the soil contains an abundance of mycorrhizal fungi, resulting in mycelial networks that connect the trees together. The trees and their seedlings can use the fungal mycelium to exchange nutrients and chemical messages.

There are two main types of mycorrhiza: ectomycorrhizae and endomycorrhizae. Ectomycorrhizae are fungi that are only externally associated with the plant root, whereas endomycorrhizae form their associations within the cells of the host. Among the mycorrhizal fungi are boletes, whose mycorrhizal relationships with larch trees (*Larix*) and other conifers have long been known. Other examples include truffles, some of which are believed to form mycorrhizae with oak (*Quercus*) or beech (*Fagus*) trees. Many orchids form mycorrhizae with species of *Rhizoctonia* that provide seedlings of the orchid host with carbohydrate obtained by degradation of organic matter in the soil.

PREDATION

A number of fungi have developed ingenious mechanisms for trapping microorganisms such as amoebas, roundworms (nematodes), and rotifers. After the prey is captured, the fungus uses hyphae to penetrate and quickly destroy the prey. Many of these fungi secrete adhesive substances over the surface of their hyphae, causing a passing animal that touches any portion of the mycelium to adhere firmly to the hyphae. For example, the mycelia of oyster mushrooms (genus *Pleurotus*) secrete adhesives onto their hyphae in order to catch nematodes. Once a passing animal is caught, a penetration tube grows out of a hypha and penetrates the host's soft body. This haustorium grows and branches and then secretes enzymes that quickly kill the animal, whose cytoplasm serves as food for the fungus.

Other fungi produce hyphal loops that ensnare small animals, thereby allowing the fungus to use its haustoria to penetrate and kill a trapped animal. Perhaps the most amazing of these fungal traps are the so-called constricting rings of some species of *Arthrobotrys*, *Dactylella*, and *Dactylaria*—soil-inhabiting fungi easily grown under laboratory conditions. In the presence of nematodes, the mycelium produces large numbers of rings through which the average nematode is barely able to pass. When anematode rubs the inner wall of a ring, which usually consists of three cells with touch-sensitive inner surfaces, the cells of the ring swell rapidly, and the resulting constriction holds the worm tightly. All efforts of the nematode to free itself fail, and a hypha, which grows out of one of the swollen ring cells at its point of contact with the worm, penetrates and branches within the animal's body, thereby killing the animal. The dead animal is then used for food by the fungus. In the absence of nematodes, these fungi do not usually produce rings in appreciable quantities. A substance secreted by nematodes stimulates the fungus to form the mycelial rings.

LICHENS

A lichen is an association between one or two fungi and an alga or cyanobacterium (blue-green alga) that results in a form distinct from either symbiont. Although lichens appear to be single plantlike organisms, under a microscope the association is seen to consist of millions of cells of algae (called the phycobiont) woven into a matrix formed of the filaments of the fungus or fungi (known as the mycobionts). The majority of mycobionts are placed in a single group of Ascomycota called the Lecanoromycetes, which are characterized by an open, often button-shaped fruit called an apothecium. The remaining mycobionts are distributed among different fungal groups. In addition to the dominant fungal symbiont, certain macrolichens also feature a basidiomycete yeast in the cortex of the organism. Although there are various types of phycobionts, half the lichen associations contain species of *Trebouxia*, a single-celled green alga. There are about 15 species of cyanobacteria that act as the photobiont in lichen associations, including some members of the genera *Calothrix*, *Gloeocapsa*, and *Nostoc*.

BASIC FEATURES

Authorities have not been able to establish with any certainty when and how fungus-alga associations evolved, although lichens must have evolved more recently than their components and probably arose independently from different groups of fungi and algae or fungi and cyanobacteria. It seems, moreover, that the ability to form lichens can spread to new groups of fungi and algae. Lichens are a biological group lacking formal status in the taxonomic framework of living organisms. Although the mycobiont(s) and phycobiont have Latin names, the product of their interaction, a lichen, does not. Earlier names given to lichens as a whole are considered names for the fungus alone. Classification of lichens is difficult and remains controversial. Part of the problem is that the taxonomy of lichens was established before their dual nature was recognized, and as a result the association was treated as a single entity.

Approximately 15,000 different kinds of lichens, some of which provide forage for reindeer and products for humans, have been described. Some lichens are leafy and form beautiful rosettes on rocks and tree trunks. Others are filamentous and drape the branches of trees, sometimes reaching a length of

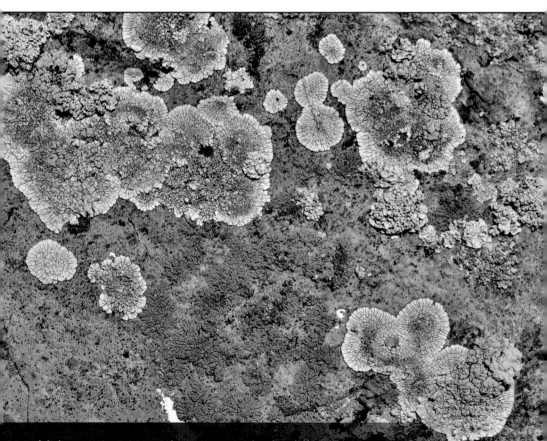

Lichens can spread across rocks in different colours and patterns.

2.75 metres (9 feet). At the opposite extreme are those smaller than a pin head and seen only with a magnifying lens. Lichens grow on almost any type of surface and can be found in almost all areas of the world. They are especially prominent in bleak, harsh regions where few plants can survive. They grow farther north and farther south and higher on mountains than most plants.

The thallus of a lichen has one of several characteristic growth forms: crustose, foliose, or fruticose. Crustose thalli, which resemble a crust closely attached to a surface, are drought-resistant and well adapted to dry climates. They prevail in deserts, Arctic and alpine regions, and ice-free parts of Antarctica. Foliose, or leafy, thalli grow best in areas of frequent rainfall. Two foliose lichens, *Hydrothyria venosa* and *Dermatocarpon fluviatile*, grow on rocks in freshwater streams of North America. Fruticose (stalked) thalli and filamentous forms prefer to utilize water in vapour form and are prevalent in humid, foggy areas such as seacoasts and mountainous regions of the tropics.

Humans have used lichens as food, as medicine, and in dyes. A versatile lichen of economic importance is *Cetraria islandica*, commonly called Iceland moss and sometimes used either as an appetite stimulant or as a foodstuff. It has also been mixed with bread and has been used to treat diabetes, nephritis, and mucus buildup. In general, however, lichens have little medical value. One lichen, *Lecanora esculenta*, is reputed to have been the manna that fell from the skies during the biblical Exodus and has served as a food source for humans and domestic animals.

Lichens are well known as dye sources. Dyes derived from them have an affinity for wool and silk and are formed by decomposition of certain lichen acids and conversion of the products. One of the best-known lichen dyes is orchil, which has a purple or red-violet colour. Orchil-producing lichens include species of *Ochrolechia*, *Roccella*, and *Umbilicaria*. Litmus, commonly made from *Lecanora tartarea* and *Roccella tinctorum*, is widely used as an acid-base indicator. Synthetic coal tar dyes, however, have replaced lichen dyes in the textile industry, and orchil is limited to use as a food-colouring agent and an acid-base indicator. A few lichens (e.g., *Evernia prunastri*) are used in the manufacture of perfumes.

Caribou and reindeer depend on lichens for two-thirds of their food supply. In northern Canada an acre of land undisturbed by animals for 120 years or more may contain 250 kg (550 pounds) of lichens. Some forage lichens that form extensive mats on the ground are *Cladonia alpestris*, *C. mitis*, *C. rangiferina*, and *C. sylvatica*. Arboreal lichens such as *Alectoria*, *Evernia*, and *Usnea* also are valuable as forage. An acre of mature black spruce trees in northern Canada, for example, may contain more than 270 kg (595 pounds) of lichens on branches within 3 metres (10 feet) of the ground.

FORM AND FUNCTION

Although the fungal symbionts of many lichens have fruiting structures on or within their thalli and may release numerous spores that develop into fungi, indirect evidence suggests that natural unions of fungi and algae occur only rarely among some lichen groups, if indeed they occur at all. In addition, free-living potential phycobionts are not widely distributed. For example, despite repeated searches, free-living populations of *Trebouxia* have not been found. This paradox, an abundance of fungal spores and a lack of algae capable of forming associations, implies that the countless spores produced by lichen fungi are functionless, at least so far as propagation of the association is concerned. Some photobionts, including species of *Nostoc* and *Trentpohlia*, can exist as free-living populations, so that natural reassociations could occur in a few lichens.

Some lichens have solved or bypassed the problem of re-forming the association. In a few lichens (e.g., *Endocarpon, Staurothele*) algae grow among the tissues of a fruiting body and are discharged along with fungal spores. Such phycobionts are called hymenial algae. When the spores germinate, the algal cells multiply and gradually form lichens with the fungus. Other lichens form structures, especially soredia, that are effective in distributing the association. A soredium, consisting of one or several algal cells enveloped by threadlike fungal filaments, or hyphae, may develop into a thallus under suitable conditions. Lichens without soredia may propagate by fragmentation of their thalli. Many lichens develop small thalloid extensions, called isidia, that also may serve in asexual propagation if broken off from the thallus.

In addition to these mechanisms for propagation, the individual symbionts have various methods of reproduction. For example, ascolichens (lichens in which the mycobiont is an ascomycete) form fruits called ascocarps that are similar to those of free-living ascomycetes, except that the mycobiont's fruits are capable of producing spores for a longer period of time. The algal symbiont within the lichen thallus reproduces by the same methods as its free-living counterpart.

Most lichen phycobionts are penetrated to varying degrees by specialized fungal structures called haustoria. *Trebouxia* lichens have a pattern in which deeply penetrating haustoria are prevalent in associations lacking a high degree of thalloid organization. On the other hand, superficial haustoria prevail among forms with highly developed thalli. *Lecanora* and *Lecidea*, for example, have individual algal cells with as many as five haustoria that may extend to the cell centre. *Alectoria* and *Cladonia* have haustoria that do not penetrate far beyond the algal cell wall. A few phycobionts, such as *Coccomyxa* and *Stichococcus*, which are not penetrated by haustoria, have thin-walled cells that are pressed close to fungal hyphae.

The flow of nutrients and metabolites between the symbionts is the basic foundation of the symbiotic system. A simple carbohydrate formed in the algal layer eventually is excreted, taken up by the mycobiont, and transformed into a different carbohydrate. The release of carbohydrate by the phycobiont and its conversion by the mycobiont occur rapidly. Whether the fungus influences the release of carbohydrate by the alga is not known with certainty, but it is known that carbohydrate excretion by the alga decreases rapidly if it is separated from the fungus.

Carbohydrate transfer is only one aspect of the symbiotic interaction in lichens. The alga may provide the fungus with vitamins, especially biotin and thiamine, important because most lichen fungi that are grown in the absence of algae have vitamin deficiencies. The alga also may contribute a substance that causes structural changes in the fungus since it forms the typical lichen thallus only in association with an alga.

One contribution of the fungus to the symbiosis

concerns absorption of water vapour from the air. The process is so effective that, at high levels of air humidity, the phycobionts of some lichens photosynthesize at near maximum rates. The upper region of a thallus provides shade for the underlying algae, some of which are sensitive to strong light. In addition, the upper region may contain pigments or crystals that further reduce light intensity and act as filters, absorbing certain wavelengths of light. Lichens synthesize a variety of unique organic compounds that tend to accumulate within the thallus. Many of these substances are coloured and are responsible for the red, yellow, or orange colour of lichens.

A lichen thallus or composite body has one of two basic structures. In a homoiomerous thallus, the algal cells, which are distributed throughout the structure, are more numerous than those of the fungus. The more common type of thallus, a heteromerous thallus, has four distinct layers, three of which are formed by the fungus and one by the alga. The fungal layers are called upper cortex, medulla, and lower cortex. The upper cortex consists of either a few layers of tightly packed cells or hyphae that may contain pigments. A cuticle may cover the cortex. The lower cortex, which is similar in structure to the upper cortex, participates in the formation of attachment structures called rhizines. The medulla, located below the algal layer, is the widest layer of a heteromerous thallus. It has a cottony appearance and consists of interlaced hyphae. The loosely structured nature of the medulla provides it with numerous air spaces and allows it to hold large amounts of water. The algal layer, about three times as wide as a cortex, consists of tightly packed algal cells enveloped by fungal hyphae from the medulla.

A heteromerous thallus may have a stalked (fruticose), crust-like (crustose), or leafy (foliose) form, and many transitional types exist. It is not known, moreover, which growth form is primitive and which is advanced. Fruticose lichens, which usually arise from a primary thallus of a different growth form (i.e., crustose, foliose), may be shrubby or pendulous or consist of upright stalks. The fruticose form usually consists of two thalloid types: the primary thallus is crust-like or lobed; the secondary thalli, which originate from the crust or lobes of the primary thallus, consist of stalks that may be simple, cup-shaped, intricately branched, and capped with brown or red fruiting bodies called apothecia. Fruticose forms such as *Usnea* may have elongated stalks with a central solid core that provides strength and elasticity to the thallus.

The crustose thallus is in such intimate contact with the surface to which it is attached that it usually cannot be removed intact. Some crustose lichens grow beneath the surface of bark or rock so that only their fruiting structures penetrate the surface.

Crustose lichens may have a hypothallus—i.e., an algal-free mat of hyphae extending beyond the margin of the regular thallus. Crustose form varies: granular types such as *Lepraria*, for example, have no organized thalloid structure; but some *Lecanora* species have highly organized thalli, with lobes that resemble foliose lichens lacking a lower cortex.

The foliose forms are flat, leaflike, and loosely attached to a surface. The largest known lichens have a foliose form; species of *Sticta* may attain a diameter of about a metre. Other common foliose genera include *Cetraria*, *Parmelia*, *Peltigera*, and *Physcia*. *Umbilicaria*, called the common rock tripe, differs from other foliose forms in its mode of attachment in that its platelike thallus attaches at the centre to a rock surface.

The complex fruiting bodies (ascocarps) of lichen fungi are of several types. The factors that induce fruiting in lichens have not been established with certainty. Spores of lichen fungi (ascospores) are of extremely varying sizes and shapes. For example, *Pertusaria* has one or two large spores in one ascus (saclike bodies containing the ascospores), and *Acarospora* may have several hundred small spores per ascus. Although in most species the ascospore generally has one nucleus, it may be single-celled or multicellular, brown or colourless. The *Pertusaria* spore, however, is a single cell containing 200 nuclei. Another type of fungal spore may be what are sometimes called spermatia (male fungal sex cells) or pycnidiospores. It is not certain that these structures have the ability to germinate and develop into a fungal colony. Few lichen fungi produce conidia, a type of asexual spore common among ascomycetes.

The metabolic activity of lichens is greatly influenced by the water content of the thallus. The rate of photosynthesis may be greatest when the amount of water in the thallus is from 65 to 90 percent of the maximum. During drying conditions, the photosynthetic rate decreases; below 30 percent it is no longer measurable. Although respiration also decreases rapidly below 80 percent water content, it persists at low rates even when the thallus is air-dried. Since lichens have no mechanisms for water retention or uptake from the surface to which they are attached, they very quickly lose the water vapour they absorb from the air. The rapid drying of lichens is a protective device since a moisture-free lichen is more resistant to temperature and light extremes than is a wet one. Frequent drying and wetting of a thallus is one of the reasons lichens have a slow growth rate.

Maximum photosynthesis in lichens takes place at temperatures of 15–20 °C (59–68 °F). More light is needed in the spring and summer than in the winter. The photosynthetic apparatus of lichens is remarkably resistant to cold temperatures. Even at temperatures below 0 °C (32°F), many lichens can absorb and fix considerable amounts of carbon dioxide. Respiration is much less at low temperatures so that, in nature, the winter months may be the most productive ones for lichens.

REPRODUCTION AND ECOLOGY OF FUNGI

The abundance and wide distribution of fungi in nature are a reflection of reproductive success and adaptation to various ecological niches. Reproduction may be either asexual or sexual. In asexual life cycles, fungi are haploid (containing one set of chromosomes), and they may use fragmentation, budding, fission, or spores to produce offspring. In sexually reproducing forms, a diploid stage occurs, in which the nuclei of the haploid sex cells fuse together, facilitating the recombination of genetic material. This provides an opportunity for the emergence of genetic variation between individuals of the same species, thereby improving the species's adaptation to the immediate environment. Certain species of fungi are very highly adapted to their habitats, requiring specific nutrients or temperature ranges for growth. Other species, however, are less tailored to their surroundings. These fungi often are able to assimilate a wide variety of organic substances and are relatively indifferent to other ecological factors such as temperature.

REPRODUCTIVE PROCESSES

Following a period of intensive growth, fungi enter a reproductive phase by forming and releasing vast quantities of spores. Spores are usually single cells produced by fragmentation of the mycelium or within specialized structures (sporangia, gametangia, sporophores, etc.). Spores may be produced either directly by asexual methods or indirectly by sexual reproduction. Sexual reproduction in fungi, as in other living organisms, involves the fusion of two nuclei that are brought together when two sex cells (gametes) unite. Asexual reproduction, which is simpler and more direct, may be accomplished by various methods.

ASEXUAL REPRODUCTION

Typically in asexual reproduction, a single individual gives rise to a genetic duplicate of the progenitor without a genetic contribution from another individual. Perhaps the simplest method of reproduction of fungi is by fragmentation of the thallus, the body of a fungus. Some yeasts, which are single-celled fungi, reproduce by simple cell division, or fission, in which one cell undergoes nuclear division and splits into two daughter cells. After some growth, these cells divide, and eventually a population of cells forms. In filamentous fungi the mycelium may fragment into a number of segments, each of which is capable of growing into a new individual. In the laboratory, fungi are commonly propagated on a layer of solid nutrient agar inoculated either with spores or with fragments of mycelium.

Budding, which is another method of asexual reproduction, occurs in most yeasts and in some filamentous fungi. In this process, a bud develops on the surface of either the yeast cell or the hypha, with the cytoplasm of the bud being continuous with that of the parent cell. The nucleus of the parent cell then divides. One of the daughter nuclei migrates into the bud, and the other remains in the parent cell. The parent cell is capable of producing many buds over its surface by continuous synthesis of cytoplasm and repeated nuclear divisions. After a bud develops to a certain point and even before it is severed from the parent cell, it is itself capable of budding by the same process. In this way, a chain of cells may be produced. Eventually, the individual buds pinch off the parent cell and become individual yeast cells. Buds that are pinched off a hypha of a filamentous fungus behave as spores; that is, they germinate, each giving rise to a structure called a germ tube, which develops into a new hypha.

Although fragmentation, fission, and budding are methods of asexual reproduction in a number of fungi, the majority reproduce asexually by the formation of spores. Spores that are produced asexually are often termed mitospores, and such spores are produced in a variety of ways.

SEXUAL REPRODUCTION

Sexual reproduction, an important source of genetic variability, allows the fungus to adapt to new environments. The process of sexual reproduction among the fungi is in many ways unique. Whereas nuclear division in other eukaryotes, such as animals, plants, and protists, involves the dissolution and re-formation of the nuclear membrane, in fungi the nuclear membrane remains intact throughout the process, although gaps in its integrity are found in some species. The nucleus of the fungus becomes pinched at its midpoint, and the diploid chromosomes are pulled apart by spindle fibres formed within the intact nucleus. The nucleolus is usually also retained and divided between the daughter cells, although it may be expelled from the nucleus, or it may be dispersed within the nucleus but detectable. Sexual reproduction in the fungi consists of three sequential stages: plasmogamy, karyogamy, and meiosis.

The diploid chromosomes are pulled apart into two daughter cells, each containing a single set of chromosomes (a haploid state). Plasmogamy, the fusion of two protoplasts (the contents of the two cells), brings together two compatible haploid nuclei. At this point, two nuclear types are present in the same cell, but the nuclei have not yet fused. Karyogamy results in the fusion of these haploid nuclei and the formation of a diploid nucleus (i.e., a nucleus containing two sets of chromosomes, one from each parent). The cell formed by karyogamy is called the zygote. In most fungi the zygote is the only cell in the entire life cycle that is diploid. The dikaryotic state that results from plasmogamy is often a prominent condition in fungi and may be prolonged over several generations. In the lower fungi, karyogamy usually follows plasmogamy almost immediately. In the more evolved fungi, however, karyogamy is separated from plasmogamy. Once karyogamy has occurred, meiosis (cell division that reduces the chromosome number to one set per cell) generally follows and restores the haploid phase. The haploid nuclei that result from meiosis are generally incorporated in spores called meiospores.

Fungi employ a variety of methods to bring together two compatible haploid nuclei (plasmogamy). Some produce specialized sex cells (gametes) that are released from differentiated sex organs called gametangia. In other fungi two gametangia come in contact, and nuclei pass from the male gametangium into the female, thus assuming the function of gametes. In still other fungi the gametangia themselves may fuse in order to bring their nuclei together. Finally, some of the most advanced fungi produce no gametangia at all. The somatic (vegetative) hyphae take over the sexual function, come in contact, fuse, and exchange nuclei.

Fungi in which a single individual bears both male and female gametangia are hermaphroditic fungi. Rarely, gametangia of different sexes are produced by separate individuals, one a male, the other a female. Such species are termed dioecious. Dioecious species usually produce sex organs only in the presence of an individual of the opposite sex.

SEXUAL INCOMPATIBILITY

Many of the simpler fungi produce differentiated male and female organs on the same thallus but do not undergo self-fertilization because their sex organs are incompatible. Such fungi require the presence of thalli of different mating types in order for sexual fusion to take place. The simplest form of this mechanism occurs in fungi in which there are two mating types, often designated + and − (or A and a). Gametes produced by one type of thallus are compatible only with gametes produced by the other type. Such fungi are said to be heterothallic. Many fungi, however, are homothallic, meaning that the sex organs produced by a single thallus are self-compatible, and a second thallus is unnecessary for sexual reproduction. Some of the most complex fungi (e.g., mushrooms) do not develop differentiated sex organs. Rather, the sexual function is carried out by their somatic hyphae, which unite and bring together compatible nuclei in preparation for fusion. Homothallism and heterothallism are encountered in fungi that have not developed differentiated sex organs, as well as in fungi in which sex organs are easily distinguishable. Compatibility therefore refers to a physiological differentiation, and sex refers to a morphological (structural) one. The two phenomena, although related, are not synonymous.

PHEROMONES

The formation of sex organs in fungi is often induced by specific organic substances. Although they were initially called sex hormones when they were first discovered, these chemicals are actually pheromones as they are produced by one partner to elicit a sexual response in the other. In *Allomyces* (order Blastocladiales) a pheromone named sirenin is secreted by the female gametes to attract the male gametes to them for fusion. In some simple fungi, which may have gametangia that are not differentiated structurally, a complex biochemical interplay between mating types produces trisporic acid, a pheromone that induces the formation of specialized aerial hyphae. Volatile intermediates in the trisporic acid synthetic pathway are interchanged between the tips of opposite mating aerial hyphae, causing the hyphae to grow toward each other and fuse together. In yeasts belonging to the phyla Ascomycota and Basidiomycota, the pheromones are small peptides. Several pheromone genes have been identified and characterized in filamentous ascomycetes and basidiomycetes.

LIFE CYCLES

In the life cycle of a sexually reproducing fungus, a haploid phase alternates with a diploid phase. The haploid phase ends with nuclear fusion, and the diploid phase begins with the formation of the zygote (the diploid cell resulting from fusion of two haploid sex cells). Meiosis (reduction division) restores the haploid number of chromosomes and initiates the haploid phase, which produced the gametes. In the majority of fungi, all structures are haploid except the zygote. Nuclear fusion takes place at the time of zygote formation, and meiosis follows immediately. Only in *Allomyces* and a few related genera and in some yeasts is the alternation of a haploid thallus with a diploid thallus definitely known.

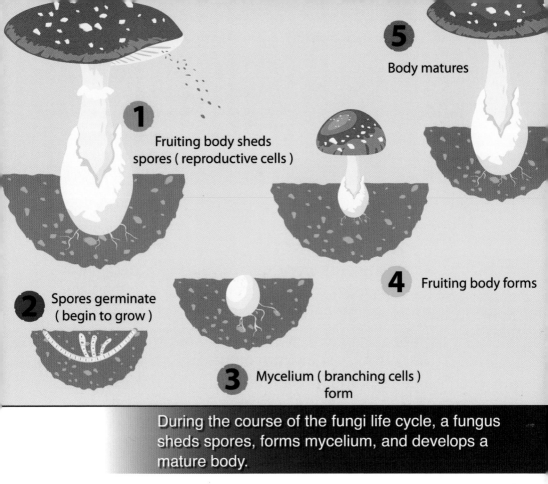

1 Fruiting body sheds spores (reproductive cells)

2 Spores germinate (begin to grow)

3 Mycelium (branching cells) form

4 Fruiting body forms

5 Body matures

During the course of the fungi life cycle, a fungus sheds spores, forms mycelium, and develops a mature body.

In the higher fungi a third condition is interspersed between the haploid and diploid phases of the life cycle. In these fungi, plasmogamy (fusion of the cellular contents of two hyphae but not of the two haploid nuclei) results in dikaryotic hyphae in which each cell contains two haploid nuclei, one from each parent. Eventually, the nuclear pair fuses to form the diploid nucleus and thus the zygote. In the Basidiomycota, binucleate cells divide successively and give rise to a binucleate mycelium, which is the main assimilative phase of the life cycle. It is the binucleate mycelium that eventually forms the basidia—the stalked fruiting bodies in which nuclear fusion and meiosis take place prior to the formation of the basidiospores.

Fungi usually reproduce both sexually and asexually. The asexual cycle produces mitospores, and the sexual cycle produces meiospores. Even though both types of spores are produced by the same mycelium, they are very different in form and easily distinguished. The asexual phase usually precedes the sexual phase in the life cycle and may be repeated frequently before the sexual phase appears.

Some fungi differ from others in their lack of one or the other of the reproductive stages. For example, some fungi reproduce only sexually (except for fragmentation, which is common in most fungi), whereas others reproduce only asexually. A number of fungi exhibit the phenomenon of parasexuality, in which processes comparable to plasmogamy, karyogamy, and meiosis take place. However, these processes do not occur at a specified time or at specified points in the life cycle of the organism. As a result, parasexuality is characterized by the prevalence of heterokaryosis in a mycelium—i.e., the presence, side by side, of nuclei of different genetic composition.

ECOLOGY

Relatively little is known of the effects of the environment on the distribution of fungi that utilize dead

RESEARCH ON FUNGI LIFE CYCLES

German botanist Heinrich Anton de Bary (1831–1888) studied the roles of fungi and other agents in causing plant diseases. His research earned him distinction as a founder of modern mycology and plant pathology. A professor of botany at the universities of Freiburg im Breisgau (1855– 66), Halle (1867–72), and Strassburg (1872–88), de Bary determined the life cycles of many fungi, for which he developed a classification that has been retained in large part by modern mycologists. Among the first to study host-parasite interactions, he demonstrated ways in which fungi penetrate host tissues.

In his book *Untersuchungen über die Brandpilze* (1853; "Researches Concerning Fungal Blights"), he correctly asserted that fungi associated with rust and smut diseases of plants are the cause, rather than the effect, of these diseases. In 1865 he proved that the life cycle of wheat rust involves two hosts, wheat and barberry. He was the first to show (1866) that lichens consist of a fungus and an alga in intimate association. He coined the term *symbiosis* in 1879 to mean an internal, mutually beneficial partnership between two organisms. De Bary also did important research on slime molds and sexual modes of reproduction in algae, and he wrote a comparative anatomy of phanerogams (plants that generate seeds) and ferns.

organic material as food (i.e., saprotrophic fungi). The availability of organic food is certainly one of the factors controlling such distribution. A great number of fungi appear able to utilize most types of organic materials, such as lignin, cellulose, or other polysaccharides, which have been added to soils or waters by dead vegetation. Most saprotrophic fungi are widely distributed throughout the world, only requiring that their habitats have sufficient organic content to support their growth. However, some sap-

Snow mold is a fungus that thrives at low temperatures.

rotrophs are strictly tropical and others are strictly temperate-zone forms. Fungi with specific nutritional requirements are even further localized.

Moisture and temperature are two additional ecological factors that are important in determining the distribution of fungi. Laboratory studies have shown that many, perhaps the majority, of fungi are mesophilic, meaning they have an optimum growth temperature of 20–30 °C (68–86 °F). Thermophilic species are able to grow at 50 °C (122 °F) or higher but are unable to grow below 30 °C. Although the optimum temperature for growth of most fungi lies at or above 20 °C, a large number of species are able to grow close to or below 0 °C (32 °F). The so-called snow molds and the fungi that cause spoilage of refrigerated foods are examples of this group. Obviously, temperature relationships influence the distribution of various species. Certain other effects of temperature are also important factors in determining the habitats of fungi. Many coprophilous (dung-inhabiting) fungi, for example, although able to grow at a temperature of 20–30 °C, require a short period at 60 °C (140 °F) for their spores to germinate.

CHAPTER

3

TYPES OF FUNGI AND LICHENS

The many different species of fungi and lichens have long fascinated scientists. By taking into account their unique shapes, sizes, mechanisms of nutrient acquisition, and genetics, mycologists have been able to arrange fungi into generalized groups known as phyla. The kingdom Fungi contains seven phyla, which separate the organisms based on broad features, such as the evolutionary histories they share with one another (phylogenetics), the structures they utilize for reproduction, the habitats they thrive within, and the relationships they have with organisms from the other kingdoms of life. For example, whereas fungi in the phylum Basidiomycota are distinguished from organisms in the phylum Ascomycota based on the shape of their spore-bearing organs, fungi in the phyla Neocallimastigomycota are distinguished from other members of the kingdom based primarily on their preferred habitat—the digestive tracts of herbivores.

Each phylum of fungi is broken down into classes, orders, families, genera, and species. As one progresses down through the system, each grouping becomes increasingly specific, ultimately separating organisms based on very fine details. The molecular characteristics of fungi, notably their DNA sequences, have been particularly important in enabling scientists to make fine distinctions between fungi. This in turn has led to the discovery of previously unknown evolutionary relationships between fungi as well as between fungi and organisms in other kingdoms.

In the first decade of the 21st century, researchers collaborating on a project known as Assembling the Fungal Tree of Life (AFTOL), funded by the U.S. National Science Foundation, expanded upon existing knowledge concerning the evolutionary histories of the different kinds of fungi. The project adopted a phylogenetic arrangement for the kingdom, thereby placing fungi into groups based largely on their evolutionary relationships, rather than solely on their morphological features. AFTOL is a work in progress, and uncertainties remain about the exact relationships of many groups. These uncertain groups are indicated in the AFTOL classification system by the term *incertae sedis*, meaning "of uncertain position," the standard term for a taxonomic group of unknown or undefined relationship. The phylogenetic classification of fungi divides the kingdom into 7 phyla, 10 subphyla, 35 classes, 12 subclasses, and 129 orders. In the coming years, as new species of fungi are discovered and evolutionary relationships are further clarified, researchers anticipate that new subclasses and orders will be added to this organization.

SELECT TYPES OF FUNGI

Of the many different types of fungi, certain groups stand out because of their unique mechanisms of reproduction, growth, and nutrient acquisition. Others are notorious pathogens, causing disease in plants and animals, or are notable for their ability to thrive in certain habitats. Among some of the best-characterized fungi are those belonging to the phyla Ascomycota and Basidiomycota.

ASCOMYCOTA

Fungi in the phylum Ascomycota (sac fungi) are characterized by a saclike structure, the ascus, which contains four to eight ascospores in the sexual stage. The sac fungi are separated into subgroups based on whether asci arise singly or are borne in one of several types of fruiting structures, or ascocarps, and on the method of discharge of the ascospores. Many ascomycetes are plant pathogens, some are animal pathogens, a few are edible mushrooms, and many live on dead organic matter (as saprotrophs).

The largest and most commonly known ascomycetes include the morel and the truffle. Other ascomycetes include important plant pathogens, such as powdery mildew of grape (*Uncinula necator*), Dutch elm disease (*Ophiostoma ulmi*), and chestnut blight (*Cryphonectria parasitica*). *Venturia inequalis* is the cause of apple scab. Perhaps the most indispensable fungus of all is an ascomycete, the common yeast (*Saccharomyces cerevisiae*), whose varieties leaven the dough in bread making and ferment grain to produce beer or mash for the distillation of alcoholic liquors. The yeast *S. cerevisiae* var. *ellipsoideus* ferments grape juice to wine.

Neurospora, a genus containing several widespread species, produces bakery mold, or red bread mold. It has been used extensively in genetic and biochemical investigations. *Xylaria* contains about 100 species of cosmopolitan fungi. One species, *X. polymorpha*, produces a club-shaped or fingerlike fruiting body (stroma) resembling burned wood and common on decaying wood or injured trees.

Cordyceps, a genus of about 400 species, are commonly known as vegetable caterpillars, or caterpillar fungi. A number of species, including *C. militaris*, parasitize insects. It forms a small, 3–4-cm

CHESTNUT BLIGHT

Chestnut blight is a plant disease caused by the fungus *Cryphonectria parasitica* (formerly known as *Endothia parasitica*). It killed virtually all the native American chestnuts (*Castanea dentata*) in the United States and Canada and also is destructive in other countries. Other blight-susceptible species include Spanish chestnut (*C. sativa*), post oak (*Quercus stellata*), and live oak (*Q. virginiana*). In Europe several oak species are affected.

Accidentally imported from Asia, the disease was first observed in 1904 in the New York Zoological Gardens. By 1925 it had decimated the American chestnut population in an area extending over 1,600 km (1,000 miles) north, south, and west of its entry point. Symptoms include reddish brown bark patches that develop into sunken or swollen and cracked cankers that kill twigs and limbs. Leaves on such branches turn brown and wither but remain attached for months. Gradually the entire tree dies. The fungus persists for years in short-lived sprouts from old chestnut roots and in less susceptible hosts. It is spread locally by splashing rain, wind, and insects; over long distances, by birds. Chinese (*C. mollissima*) and Japanese (*C. crenata*) chestnuts are resistant. Crosses between American and Asian species have produced varieties with excellent nuts, but timber quality is closely linked with blight susceptibility. In the 1970s a native American strain of chestnut blight was identified. Experiments indicated that the native strain was less virulent than other strains and that it had a nullifying effect on lethal strains. Unfortunately, the mild strain of blight does not readily spread from tree to tree among American chestnuts.

(about 1 1/3-inch) mushroomlike fruiting structure with a bright orange head, or cap. A related genus, *Claviceps*, includes *C. purpurea*, the cause of ergot of rye and ergotism in humans and domestic animals. Earth tongue is the common name for *Geoglossum* species. They produce black to brown, club-shaped fruiting structures on soil or decaying wood.

Cup Fungi

Cup fungi form a large group of Ascomycetes in the order Pezizales. They typically are characterized by a disk- or cup-shaped structure (apothecium) bearing spore sacs (asci) on its surface. Some of the cup fungi are important plant pathogens, such as *Monilinia* (*Sclerotinia*), causing brown rot in peach and other stone fruits. Others are saprotrophs, displaying small (2–5 mm [0.08–0.2 inch]), brilliant red or orange disks found on old cow dung and decaying twigs and branches.

Cookeina tricholoma is a cup fungus that grows in tropical and subtropical regions.

Each ascus usually contains eight ascospores. Apothecia are usually open to the exterior. However, in subterranean truffles, the apothecia are completely enclosed, exposed only when the truffle is opened. Many of the cup fungi produce ballistospores, ascospores that are forcibly shot out. Sometimes, as in *Helvella* and *Peziza*, they are discharged in such numbers that they form a cloud above the fruiting body, and innumerable tiny explosions may be heard as a hissing sound.

The term *morel* is used for the species of edible *Morchella* mushrooms. They have a convoluted or pitted head, or cap. Morels are varied in shape and occur in diverse habitats. The edible *M. esculenta* is found during early summer in woods. The bell morel (*Verpa*), an edible mushroom with a bell-shaped cap, is found in woods and in old orchards in early spring. Most species of *Gyromitra*, a genus of false morels, are poisonous. One species, *G. brunnea*, is edible, however, and is found in sandy soils or woods.

Peziza, which contains about 50 widespread species, produce a cup-shaped fruiting body or mushroomlike structure on rotting wood or manure. Fire fungus is the common name for two genera (*Pyronema* and *Anthracobia*) that grow on burned wood or soil.

The edible snow mushroom (*Helvella gigas*) is found at the edge of melting snow in some localities. Caution is advised for all *Helvella* species as some are considered poisonous. One such fungus, *H. infula*, has a dull yellow to bay-brown, saddle-shaped cap. It grows on rotten wood and rich soil from late summer to early fall and is poisonous to some people. *Sarcoscypha* and *Geopyxis* (earth cup) are typically cupor goblet-shaped.

EUROTIOMYCETES

Eurotiomycetes is a class of fungi in the phylum Ascomycota. The members of Eurotiomycetes produce asci containing ascospores in either a closed fruiting body (ascocarp) or spore balls. Example genera are *Capronia* (order Chaetothyriales), which includes some marine fungi; *Pyrenula* (order Pyrenulales), which includes wart lichens; and *Eurotium* (order Eurotiales).

ASPERGILLUS

Aspergillus is a genus of molds in the order Eurotiales. These organisms usually exist as asexual forms (or anamorphs) and are pathogenic in humans. About one-third of *Aspergillus* species are known to have a sexual phase. *Aspergillus niger* causes black mold of foodstuffs and, together with *A. fumigatus*, is the cause of aspergillosis in humans. Sake is fermented with *A. oryzae*, and soybeans are processed with *A. wentii*. Three other genera have *Aspergillus*-type conidia (asexually produced spores): *Emericella*, *Eurotium*, and *Sartorya*.

PENICILLIUM

Penicillium is a genus of blue or green mold fungi that exists as asexual forms (anamorphs, or deuteromycetes). Those species for which the sexual phase is known are placed in the order Eurotiales. Found on foodstuffs, leather, and fabrics, they are of economic importance in the production of antibiotics, organic acids, and cheeses.

Penicillin, the first and still one of the most widely used antibiotic agents, was derived from *Penicillium* mold in 1928 by Scottish bacteriologist Sir Alexander Fleming. Fleming observed that colonies of the bacterium *Staphylococcus aureus* failed to grow in those areas of a culture that had been accidentally contaminated by the green mold *Penicillium notatum*. He isolated the mold, grew it in a fluid medium, and found that it produced a substance capable of killing many of the common bacteria that infect humans. Australian pathologist Howard Florey and British biochemist Ernst Boris Chain isolated and purified penicillin in the late 1930s, and by 1941 an injectable form of the drug was available for therapeutic use.

The several kinds of penicillin synthesized by various species of the mold *Penicillium* may be divided into two classes: the naturally occurring penicillins (those formed during the process of mold fermentation) and the semisynthetic penicillins (those in which the structure of a chemical substance—6-aminopenicillanic acid—found in all penicillins is altered in various ways). Because it is possible to change the characteristics of the antibiotic, different types of penicillin are produced for different therapeutic purposes. Penicillin G is the only naturally occurring penicillin that is still used clinically. Because of its poor stability in acid, much of penicillin G is broken down as it passes through the stomach. As a result of this characteristic, it must be given by intramuscular injection, which limits its usefulness. Some of the semisynthetic penicillins are more acid-stable and thus may be given as oral medication.

All penicillins work in the same way—namely, by inhibiting the bacterial enzymes responsible for cell wall synthesis and by activating other enzymes to break down the protective wall of the microorganism. Therefore, they are not effective against microorganisms that do not produce cell walls. Some strains of previously susceptible bacteria, such as *Staphylococcus*, have developed a specific resistance to the naturally occurring penicillins. These bacteria either produce β-lactamase (penicillinase), an enzyme that disrupts the internal structure of penicillin and thus destroys the antimicrobial action of the drug, or they lack cell wall receptors for penicillin, greatly reducing the ability of the drug to enter bacterial cells. This has led to the production of the penicillinase-resistant penicillins.

Penicillins are used in the treatment of throat infections, meningitis, syphilis, and various other infections. The chief side effects of penicillin are hypersensitivity reactions, including skin rash, hives, swelling, and anaphylaxis, or allergic shock. The more serious reactions are uncommon. Milder symptoms may be treated with corticosteroids but usually are prevented by switching to alternative antibiotics. Anaphylactic shock, which can occur in previously sensitized individuals within seconds or minutes, may require immediate administration of epinephrine.

Sᴏʀᴅᴀʀɪᴏᴍʏᴄᴇᴛᴇꜱ

Sordariomycetes is a class of several thousand species of sac fungi in the phylum Ascomycota. These fungi are characterized by a flask-shaped fruiting body (perithecium) that bears asci and usually has a pore (ostiole) through which ascospores are discharged. Genera that parasitize higher plants include *Ophiostoma* (Dutch elm disease), *Gnomonia* (leaf spots), *Diaporthe* (stem and leaf blights), *Claviceps* (ergot of rye), and those of the powdery mildew fungi. Fungal genetics have been extensively studied in *Glomerella*.

Tʀᴜꜰꜰʟᴇꜱ

Truffles are edible, subterranean fungi. They have been prized as a food delicacy from Classical times. Truffles are in the genus *Tuber*, order Pezizales (phylum Ascomycota). They are native mainly to temperate regions. The different species range in size from that of a pea to that of an orange. The white, homogeneous flesh of young truffles usually ages to become a rich, dark colour with lighter marbling. Truffles flourish in open woodland on calcareous soil. They are saprotrophs, usually associated with the roots of trees, possibly in a mutually beneficial association. The spores of *Tuber* are large, and from one to four may be seen in a spore sac, or ascus. (These, the first ascospores to be observed, were described by French botanist Joseph Pitton de Tournefort in 1701–11.) The most valued truffle in French cookery is the Périgord (*T. melanosporum*), which is said to have first gained favour toward the end of the 15th century. It is brown or black, rounded, and covered with polygonal warts having a depression at their

Truffle hunters like this one in northern Italy use dogs to sniff out the valuable edible fungi.

summit. The flesh (gleba) is first white, then brown or gray, and when mature becomes black with white veins having a brown margin. The odour is well marked and pleasant. The main French *truffières* (truffle grounds) are in Périgord and the *département* of Vaucluse, though truffles are gathered throughout a large part of France.

The truffle industry is an important one in France, and about one-third of the gatherings are exported. The French government undertook the reforesting of many large and barren areas, for many of the best truffle regions become productive by the planting of trees, particularly oaks. Because truffles often occur at depths of up to about 30 cm (12 inches), it is difficult to detect them unaided. Truffles, when occurring near the surface of the ground, crack it as they reach full size, and experienced gatherers can detect them. Furthermore, in the morning and evening columns of small yellow flies may be seen hovering over a colony. Occasionally an individual is sufficiently sensitive to the scent of truffles to locate them, but truffle hunting is usually carried on with the aid of trained pigs and dogs.

Although truffles are much desired as food, direct cultivation of truffles for commerce is difficult. Calcareous ground is dug over and acorns or seedlings planted. Soil from truffle areas is usually spread about, and the ground is kept in condition by light plowing and harrowing. After three years, clearings are made and the trees pruned. If they are to appear, truffles do so only after about five years. Gathering begins then, but is not very profitable until 8 or 10 years have passed. The yield is at its maximum from 5 to 25 years later.

The English truffle, *T. aestivum*, is found principally in beech woods. It is bluish black, rounded, and covered with coarse polygonal warts. The gleba is white when immature, then yellowish, and finally brown with white branched markings. Truffles are rare in North America, being found most often in Oregon and California. False truffles (genus *Rhizopogon*, order Boletales, phylum Basidiomycota) form small, underground, potato-like structures under coniferous trees in parts of North America.

YEAST

Yeast are any of certain economically important single-celled fungi, most of which are in the phylum Ascomycota, only a few being Basidiomycota. Yeasts are found worldwide in soils and on plant surfaces and are especially abundant in sugary mediums such as flower nectar and fruits. There are hundreds of varieties of ascomycete yeasts. The types commonly used in the production of bread, beer, and wine are selected strains of *Saccharomyces cerevisiae*. The small cakes and packets of yeast used in food and beverage-processing contain billions of individual yeast cells, each about 0.075 mm (0.003 inch) in diameter.

Yeasts reproduce asexually by budding: a small bump protrudes from a parent cell, enlarges, matures, and detaches. A few yeasts reproduce by fission, the parent cell dividing into two equal cells. Some yeasts are mild to dangerous pathogens of humans and other animals (e.g., *Candida albicans*, *Histoplasma*, *Blastomyces*). *Torula* is a genus of wild yeasts that are imperfect, meaning they never form sexual spores.

In food manufacture, yeast is used to cause fermentation and leavening. The fungi feed on sugars, producing alcohol (ethanol) and carbon dioxide. In beer and wine manufacture the former is the desired product, in baking, the latter. In sparkling wines and beer some of the carbon dioxide is retained in the finished beverage. The alcohol produced in bread making is driven off when the dough is baked. The fermentation of wine is initiated by naturally occurring yeasts present in the vineyards. One yeast cell can ferment approximately its own weight of glucose per hour.

Yeast is 50 percent protein and is a rich source of vitamins B_1 and B_2 niacin, and folic acid. Brewer's yeast is sometimes eaten as a vitamin supplement. In commercial production, selected strains of yeast are fed a solution of molasses, mineral salts, and ammonia. When growth ceases, the yeast is separated from the nutrient solution, washed, and packaged. Yeast for baking is sold in compressed cakes containing starch or in a dry granular form mixed with cornmeal.

BASIDIOMYCOTA

Basidiomycota is a large and diverse phylum of fungi that includes jelly and shelf, or bracket, fungi; mushrooms, puffballs, and stinkhorns; and the rusts and smuts. The club-shaped spore-bearing organ (basidium) usually produces four sexual spores (basidiospores). Basidia are borne on fruiting bodies (basidiocarps), which are large and conspicuous in all but the rusts and smuts.

The common name bird's nest fungus includes species of the genera *Crucibulum*, *Cyathus*, and *Nidularia* of the family Nidulariaceae (order Agaricales), which contains about 60 species. The hollow fruiting body resembles a nest containing eggs (peridioles). The peridioles carry the spores when they disperse at maturity.

Many species of the subphylum Pucciniomycotina do not form fruiting bodies. The species, parasitic on higher plants, cause leaf spots, witches'-broom (tufted growth), and galls (swellings). Particularly affected are azaleas and rhododendrons. The Pucciniomycotina include smut fungi.

Jelly fungus is the common name for several species of the cosmopolitan order Tremellales, including those of the genus *Tremella* (40 species), and are so called because of their jelly-like fruiting bodies. Frequently brightly coloured (especially yellow and orange) or white, the fungi occur on decaying wood after heavy rains in late summer.

The ear fungus (*Auricularia auricula-judae*) is a brown, gelatinous edible fungus found on dead tree trunks in moist weather in the autumn. One of 10

Auricularia auricula-judae is a fungus that often bears a striking resemblance to the shape of a human ear.

widespread *Auricularia* species, it is ear- or shell-shaped and sometimes acts as a parasite, especially on elder (*Sambucus*).

AGARICALES

Agaricales is an order of fungi in the class Agaricomycetes (phylum Basidiomycota). Traditionally, agarics were classified based on the presence of gills (thin sheets of spore-bearing cells, or basidia) and mushroom-shaped fruiting bodies. Today, agarics are classified based on genetic relatedness, and thus they may or may not have gills, and fruiting bodies may or may not be mushroom-shaped. The best known family, Agaricaceae, has basidia located on gills. The familiar commercially grown mushroom is a representative example: its fruiting structure (the mushroom proper) typically consists of a stalk (stipe) and a cap (pileus), which bears the gills on its underside. Best known of the agarics is the genus *Agaricus*, with more than 200 species. The most prominent of the agarics are the edible meadow or field mushroom *A. campestris* and the common cultivated mushroom *A. bisporus*. The family Amanitaceae contains many species that are poisonous.

Among the remaining families, the following members are of interest. *Clitocybe* is a cosmopolitan genus and contains the poisonous *C. illudens*, the jack-o-lantern, which glows in the dark. This orange-yellow fungus of woods and stumps resembles the sought after edible species of *Cantharellus*, the chanterelle. The similarity emphasizes the need for careful identification by the mushroom gatherer. *Russula* has about 750 species, many with caps of red, orange, yellow, or green. *Lactarius* has milky (hence the name) or bluish juice. The genus contains the edible *L. deliciosus* as well as several poisonous species. *Coprinus*, the ink caps, characteristically grow in clumps at the sides of roads and at the base of old stumps. They are characterized by bullet-shaped caps, black spores (which make the gills appear black), and their habit of liquefying when mature, leaving an inky mass. The majority are edible, a few are somewhat poisonous, and some are mildly toxic only when alcoholic beverages are consumed with the mushrooms.

Armillaria is a genus of about 35 cosmopolitan species. The edible honey mushroom, *A. mellea*, causes root rot in trees. Its yellowish clusters are often found at the bases of trees and stumps, and black, shoestring-like fungal filaments can be found in the decaying wood. *Armillaria ponderosa*, an edible mushroom with an interesting cinnamon flavor, is found in Northwest coastal forests. It is avidly collected by Japanese-Americans, who call it matsutake, after the matsutake of Japan (*Tricholoma matsutake*). *Tricholoma* also contains a number of inedible forms, including the very poisonous *T. pardinum*.

Pholiota is found almost exclusively on wood. Some species are known to cause heartwood rot in trees. The cap and stalk of *P. squarrosa*, an edible mushroom, are covered with dense, dry scales. Among the shelf or bracket fungi growing from tree trunks is the oyster cap, *Pleurotus ostreatus*, so called because of its appearance. It is edible when young, but, as with most shelf and bracket fungi, it tends to become hard or leathery with age. The small *Marasmius oreades* appears frequently in lawns.

The Agaricales order also includes the families Schizophyllaceae and Fistulinaceae, which were formerly placed in the order Polyporales. *Schizophyllum commune*, a very common and widespread white mushroom, grows on decaying wood and has a cap with split gills that roll inward to cover the hymenium in dry weather. *Fistulina hepatica*, commonly called beefsteak fungus, is an edible species found in the autumn on oaks and other trees, on which it causes a stain called brown oak. Its common name is derived from its colour, which resembles that of raw beef.

AMANITA

Amanita is a genus of more than 600 species of mushrooms in the family Amanitaceae (order Agaricales). Some species of *Amanita* are poisonous to humans. The amanitas typically have white spores, a ring on the stem slightly below the cap, a veil (volva) torn as the cap expands, and a cup from which the stalk arises.

Among the deadliest of all mushrooms are the destroying angels (*A. bispongera*, *A. ocreata*, *A. verna*, and *A. virosa*). They develop a large white fruiting body and are found in forests during wet periods in summer and autumn. Death cap (*A. phalloides*), also deadly, is found in woods or their borders. It has a green or brown cap and appears in summer or early autumn. Other poisonous species include *A. brunnescens* and *A. pantherina*. Common edible species include *A. caesarea*, *A. rubescens*, and *A. vaginata*. The fly agaric, or fly amanita (*A. muscaria*), is a poisonous mushroom found in pastures and fields in summer. It was once used as a fly poison.

ARMILLARIA

Armillaria is a genus of fungi in the order Agaricales (phylum Basidiomycota). Species of *Armillaria* are found throughout northern North America and Europe, principally in forests of hardwoods or mixed conifers. In suitable environments, members of this genus may live for hundreds of years, and certain specimens have been identified as among the largest and oldest living organisms.

From late summer to autumn, *Armillaria* species produce similar-looking mushrooms, or fruiting bodies, with notched gills extending part way down the stalk and a single or double ring near the base of the cap. The colour ranges from white to golden. Most species are found on the ground, but a few, including the honey mushroom (*A. mellea*), will grow directly on wood.

Armillaria grow from a single fertilized white spore and spread vegetatively through hyphae, threadlike filaments of cells that aggregate to form long, cord-like bundles called rhizomorphs. The rhizomorphs' underground growth may form an extensive network, or mat, as it spreads through the soil in search of nutrients from decaying wood or living tree roots. The rhizomorphs secrete enzymes that digest these foods, which are absorbed through the hyphal walls. Shielded underground, the hardy rhizomorph can withstand extremes of temperature, including aboveground forest fires.

Given suitable forest conditions, the fungal mat (mycelium) can reach extraordinary proportions. In 1992 a mat of *A. bulbosa* was identified in a mixed oak forest near Crystal Falls, in Michigan's Upper Peninsula. Genetic testing on sample mushrooms gathered throughout the area determined that all were produced by a single supporting mycelium that extended over more than

15 hectares (37 acres). Its estimated total weight was more than 10,000 kg (220,000 pounds), and, based on calculations from known growth rates, it was thought to be at least 1,500 years old. Later that year, a specimen of *A. ostoyae* was identified on Mount Adams, in southwestern Washington state. Its age was estimated at 400 to 1,000 years, and it far exceeded the Michigan fungus in size, covering some 607 hectares (1,500 acres).

LYCOPERDACEAE

Lycoperdaceae is a family of fungi in the order Agaricales (phylum Basidiomycota) that includes about 160 species, among them earthstars and puffballs, which are found in soil or on decaying wood in grassy areas and woods. Many puffballs, named for the features of the fruiting body (basidiocarp), are edible before maturity, at which time the internal tissues become dry and powdery. Puffs of spores discharge when the fruiting structure is disturbed. *Calbovista subsculpta*, an edible puffball, is found along old road beds and in pastures.

Lycoperdon is a genus of 50 cosmopolitan species of small common puffballs. One species, *L. perlatum* (*L. gemmatum*), has spotlike scars on the surface and is edible only when young. These fungi are found in the woods or on sawdust in summer and autumn.

Calvatia is a genus of about 35 species that are especially common in temperate regions. The giant puffball (*C. gigantea*), edible while young and white inside, is found in late summer on wet humus or soil. The fruiting body may be as large as 120 cm (4 feet) across and contains over ten trillion spores. Another genus is *Geastrum* (*Geaster*), consisting of about 50 widespread species of earthstars with an expanded starlike base. They are found among dead leaves in woods in summer and autumn.

A related group of puffballs and earthstars, the Sclerodermataceae, is placed within the order Boletales. Individuals of these species, found in soil and rotting wood, form puffball-like fruiting bodies with a hard outer wall and a dark-coloured interior when mature.

BOLETALES

Boletales is a diverse order of fungi in the class Agaricomycetes (phylum Basidiomycota) that includes some boletes, earthballs, puffballs, and false truffles. Most members are saprotrophic, primarily found on the wood of fallen trees or in the soil at the base of trees. The fruiting structures of members of family Boletaceae bear pores rather than gills (as in the Agaricales). Some edible mushrooms are included in the family's more than 250 cosmopolitan species. They usually can be found in the woods during hot, rainy periods.

Examples of genera in the order Boletales are *Rhizopogon* (150 species widespread in North America) and *Boletus*. Several of the 50 species of the genus *Boletus* are edible. The undersurfaces range from red to brown in colour. The cepe (*B. edulis*) is found in woods and groves of trees during July and August. The 50 species of *Suillus* form mycorrhizal associations between the filaments of the fungus and the roots of certain trees.

POLYPORALES

Polyporales is a large order of pore fungi within the phylum Basidiomycota. The 2,300 known species have conspicuous sporophores (fruiting bodies), sometimes mushroomlike, the spore-bearing layer (hymenium) appearing either tube-shaped, gill-like, rough, smooth, or convoluted. Many species are found on the ground or on decaying wood. Some species are edible, and others cause diseases of trees.

The order includes the shelf, or bracket, fungi (Polyporaceae), which produces a shelflike fruiting structure on many trees. They cause decay of birch and other hardwoods and of structural timbers (certain *Poria* species); conifer rot, heart rot, and root rot of rubber plants (*Fomes*); wood decay and root rot of cacao, coffee, rubber, and other trees (*Ganoderma*); and diseases of birch and conifers (*Polyporus*). The white undersurface of artist's fungus (*Ganoderma applanatum*), which darkens when cut, has been used for etching.

The inedible birch fungus *Polyporus betulinus* causes decay on birch trees in the northern United States. Dryad's saddle (*P. squamosus*) produces a fanor saddle-shaped mushroom. It is light coloured with dark scales, has a strong odour, and grows on many deciduous trees. The edible hen of the woods (*Grifola frondosus*), which grows on old trees and stumps, produces a cluster of grayish mushrooms with two or three caps on a stalk; the undersides of the caps are porous. The edible chicken of the woods, *Laetiporus sulphureus*, is a common, shelf-like fungus that grows on dead wood. It derives its Latin name from its sulfur-yellow colour. Only the younger portions of the fruiting body are edible.

CHYTRIDIOMYCOTA

Chytridiomycota is a phylum of fungi, members of which are distinguished by having zoospores (motile cells) with a single, posterior, whiplash structure (flagellum). Species are microscopic in size, and most are found in freshwater or wet soils. Most are parasites of algae and animals or live on organic debris (as saprotrophs). A few species in the order Chytridiales cause plant disease, and one species, *Batrachochytrium dendrobatidis*, has been shown to cause disease in frogs and amphibians.

MICROSPORIDIA

Microsporidia is a group of parasitic organisms that under some taxonomic systems is placed among the fungi and under other systems is placed among the protists. Microsporidians are found mainly in cells of the gut epithelium of insects and the skin and muscles of fish. They also occur in annelids and some other invertebrates. Infection is characterized by enlargement of the affected tissue. Microsporidians have minute spores (2 to 20 micrometres, or 0.00008 to 0.0008 inch) that contain a single polar filament and the infective parasite (sporoplasm). When spores are ingested by a new host, the organisms enter the gut epithelium and reach specific tissues through the bloodstream or the body cavity. In the host cells they grow and repeatedly divide asexually. The mature parasites (trophozoites) eventually give rise to sexually produced zygotes that produce new spores.

The genus *Nosema* contains parasitic spore-forming organisms. These organisms are found in host cells where they undergo repeated asexual divisions followed by spore formation. The species *N. bombycis*, which causes the epidemic disease pébrine in silkworms, attacks all tissues and all developmental stages from embryo to adult. In advanced infections, small brown spots cover the body of the silkworm. Diseased larvae, which either are unable to spin cocoons or else spin them loosely, die without pupating. French chemist and microbiologist Louis Pasteur identified the spores ("corpuscles") of *Nosema* as the disease agent in 1865 and suggested control by destruction of infected silkworm colonies and improved sanitation.

OOMYCOTA

Oomycota is a phylum of fungus-like organisms in the kingdom Chromista that is distinguished by the organisms' production of large, spherical oogonia, or female eggs. The Oomycota reproduce asexually by zoospores, which move through the use of one or two flagella. New individuals may germinate from these spores, or mature individuals may reproduce sexually, with the resulting fertilized eggs being converted into nonmobile spores, or oospores, which then also germinate into mature individuals. Oomycetes may occur as saprotrophs (living on decayed matter) or as parasites living on higher plants. Among the various aquatic, amphibious, or terrestrial species, one played an important role in modern history: the species *Phytophthora infestans* destroyed Ireland's potato crop and caused the famine of 1845, which resulted in a mass migration of the Irish to the United States. Some other economically destructive genera include *Saprolegnia* (water molds), *Aphanomyces* (the cause of root rot of pea), and *Plasmopara* (downy mildews).

LATE BLIGHT

Late blight is a disease of potato and tomato plants that is caused by the fungus-like water mold *Phytophthora infestans*. The disease occurs in humid regions with temperature ranges of between 4 and 29 °C (40 and 80 °F); hot, dry weather checks its spread. Potato or tomato vines that are infected may rot within two weeks. The Irish potato famines of the mid-19th century were caused by late blight. The disease destroyed more than half of the tomato crop in the eastern United States in 1946, leading to the establishment of a blight-forecasting service in 1947. Although forecasting has helped to prevent massive outbreaks of the disease, the mold continues to be a problem for tomato and potato farmers in the 21st century.

When plants have become infected, lesions (round or irregularly shaped areas that range in colour from dark green to purplish black and resemble frost injury) appear on the leaves, petioles, and stems. A whitish growth of spore-produced structures may appear at the margin of the lesions on the underleaf surfaces. Potato tubers develop rot up to 15 mm (0.6 inch) deep. Secondary fungi and bacteria (*Erwinia* species) often invade potato tubers and produce rotting that results in great losses during storage, transit, and marketing.

Phytophthora survives in stored tubers, dump piles, field plants, and greenhouse tomatoes. Sporangia are airborne to nearby plants, in which infection may occur within a few hours. At temperatures

(continued on the next page)

Late blight, seen in this tomato, is difficult to treat. Farmers and gardeners can attempt to avert it by paying attention to weather conditions, giving plants sufficient space, and avoiding overwatering.

(continued from the previous page)

below 15 °C (59 °F) sporangia germinate by producing zoospores that encyst and later form a germ tube. Above that temperature most sporangia produce a germ tube directly. Foliage blighting and a new crop of sporangia are produced within four to six days after infection. The cycle is repeated as long as cool, moist weather prevails. Another species, *N. apis*, attacks the gut epithelium of honeybees (especially workers) and causes nosema disease, a serious form of dysentery in animals.

SELECT TYPES OF LICHENS

There exist numerous different types of lichens, involving a variety of fungus-alga associations. Lichens are generally recognized by common names, such as beard lichen and Iceland moss. Some of the best-characterized lichens are those that are used by humans as sources of foods or dyes.

BEARD LICHEN

Beard lichen is any member of the genus *Usnea*. It is a yellow or greenish fruticose (bushy, branched) lichen with long stems and disk-shaped holdfasts, which resembles a tangled mass of threads. It occurs in both the Arctic and the tropics, where it is eaten by wild animals or collected as fodder. In the past it was used as a remedy for whooping cough, catarrh, epilepsy, and dropsy. It has been used also as an astringent, a tonic, and a diuretic. Old-man's-beard (*U. barbata*) was first described in 300 BCE as a hair-growth stimulant. Hanging moss (*U. longissima*) looks like gray threads about 1.5 metres (5 feet) long hanging from tree branches in humid, mountainous regions. Some species of *Usnea* also produce an orange dye. It is the "beard moss," or "tree moss," of the poets and Shakespeare's "idle moss." It is sometimes confused with

Lichens of the genus *Usnea* are known as beard lichen because they can resemble a beard as they dangle from a branch or twig.

the plant known as Spanish moss, which is similar in appearance but is unrelated to lichens.

ICELAND MOSS

Iceland moss (*Cetraria islandica*) is a fruticose lichen with an upright thallus usually attached in one place. It varies in colour from deep brown to grayish white and may grow to a height of 7 cm (3 inches). The trough-shaped branches fork into flattened lobes that are edged with short hairs. Iceland moss grows in alpine areas of the Northern Hemisphere and on the lava slopes and plains of Iceland, whence it received its name. It is an important food for reindeer, caribou, musk-oxen, and moose. Iceland moss is also used as a food supplement for sheep and cattle and was probably the first lichen used as food by humans. It is soaked, dried, powdered, and mixed with cereals and potatoes for use in breads, soups, salads, and jellies. Slightly bitter-tasting, it contains about 70 percent lichenin, a lichen starch, and an extractable brown dye. Because Iceland moss is a source of glycerol, it is used in the soap industry and in the manufacture of cold creams.

OAK MOSS

Oak moss (*Evernia prunastri*) is a species of fruticose lichen valued in perfumery for its heavy, oriental fragrance and as a fixative base. It grows in mountainous areas throughout much of the Northern Hemisphere. The pale greenish gray thallus, 3 to 8 cm (1.2 to 3 inches) long, is palmately branched, ending in pointed tips. The upper surface is green and warty with pale gray reproductive bodies (soredia). The undersurface is whitish with a faint netlike pattern. A less common species (*E. furfuracea*), having similar properties, is often included under the same common name, which is a translation of the French *mousse de chêne*.

Oak moss was used in perfumery as early as the 16th century. Baskets filled with it have been found in the ancient royal tombs of Egypt, but whether it was intended for perfume or for food is not known. Oak moss contains a starchy edible substance. A mixture of acids extracted from it is used in drugs for treating external wounds and infections.

PARMELIA

Parmelia is the largest genus of foliose lichens, which includes among its members the species commonly known as crottle and skull lichen. Crottle, the largest foliose lichen, resembles crumpled leather and sometimes grows 90 to 120 cm (35 to 47 inches) in diameter. It is characterized by a black underside. The central portion may die out, leaving a toadstool-like fairy ring. It is used as a reddish brown cloth dye and was once considered a cure for epilepsy and the plague. The so-called skull lichen is a common variety that grows in flat gray-brown rosettes (5 to 10 cm [2 to 4 inches] across). According to folk superstition, it was believed to be an effective treatment for epilepsy if found growing on an old skull, especially that of an executed criminal.

CHAPTER

4

FEATURES OF PROTISTS

I n 1866 German zoologist Ernst Haeckel proposed the establishment of the kingdom Protista to embrace "lower" organisms. However,
his conception failed to gain widespread support
during his lifetime. Much later, in the 1970s and
'80s, the work of American biologists R.H. Whittaker
and Lynn Margulis, as well as others, led to widespread support for considering living organisms as
constituting five separate kingdoms, one of which
was kingdom Protista. This grouping consisted of
eukaryotic, predominantly unicellular microscopic
organisms known generally as protozoans, algae,
and "fungi-like" organisms, though some scientists
now reject it as too general.

Protists often share certain morphological and physiological characteristics with animals, plants, and fungi. However, protists are neither animals nor plants, nor are they fungi. In fact, although the protists were given their own kingdom, recent genetic and biochemical studies have demonstrated that many of the traditional members of the kingdom do not share a common evolutionary history. Thus,

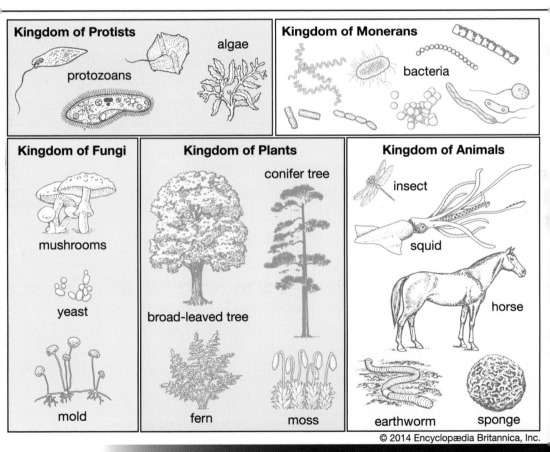

Kingdom of Protists — protozoans, algae

Kingdom of Monerans — bacteria

Kingdom of Fungi — mushrooms, yeast, mold

Kingdom of Plants — conifer tree, broad-leaved tree, fern, moss

Kingdom of Animals — insect, squid, horse, earthworm, sponge

© 2014 Encyclopædia Britannica, Inc.

R.H. Whittaker's classification of life into five kingdoms is now considered problematic because of the diversity of features among protists, among other challenges.

despite the work of Whittaker and Margulis, most scientists have abandoned the use of kingdom Protista in formal classification schemes.

Because of their somewhat ambiguous and diverging evolutionary histories, protists are extraordinarily heterogeneous, far more so than fungi and lichens. This diversity can be seen in the various ways in which they acquire nutrients, whether through the breakdown of organic matter or through symbiosis, parasitism, photosynthesis, or other types of interactions with plants and animals. Many protists are motile, often having either flagella, cilia, or pseudopodia, which allow them to navigate within aqueous habitats. Many protists are pathogenic (disease-causing) in plants or animals, and some cause serious diseases—such as malaria and sleeping sickness—in humans. Thus, although the protists are no longer recognized as a formal group in current biological classification systems, they still are important members of life on Earth.

Among the major groups of free-living protists are the ciliates, the amoebae, the heterokonts (e.g., golden algae, brown algae, and diatoms), the chlorophytes (green algae), and the excavates (e.g., euglena and trypanosomes). These groups of organisms are important ecologically for their role in the microbial carbon and nutrient cycles and are found in a wide variety of habitats, from terrestrial soils to freshwater and marine environments to sediments and sea ice.

GENERAL FEATURES

The protists include all unicellular organisms not included with the prokaryotes (with the exception of yeast, which are grouped with the fungi). Protists also embrace a number of forms of syncytial (coenocytic) or multicellular composition, generally manifest as filaments, colonies, coenobia (a type of colony with a fixed number of interconnected cells embedded in a common matrix before release from the parental colony), or thalli (a leaflike, multicellular structure or body composed primarily of a single undifferenti- ated tissue). Not all protists are microscopic. Some groups have large species indeed. For example, among the brown algal protists some forms may reach a length of 60 metres (about 200 feet) or more. A common range in body length, however, is from a few micrometres to a few millimetres.

Some parasitic forms (e.g., the malarial organ- isms) and a few free-living algal protists may have a diameter, or length, of only 1 micrometre (0.000039 inch). While members of many protist groups are capable of motility, primarily by means of flagella (whiplike extrusions), cilia (hairlike extrusions), or pseudopodia ("false feet" or temporarily protruding sections of a single-celled organism), other groups (or certain members of the groups) may be nonmo- tile for most or part of the life cycle. Resting stages (spores or cysts) are common among many taxa, and modes of nutrition include photosynthesis, absorption, and ingestion. Some species exhibit both autotrophic and heterotrophic nutrition (autotrophs utilize inorganic compounds as sources of nutrients, and heterotrophs utilize organic compounds for nutrients). The great diversity shown in protist characteristics supports the theories about the antiquity of the protists and of the ancestral role they play with respect to the other eukaryotic groups.

The architectural complexity of most protist cells is what sets them apart from the cells of plant and animal tissues. Unicellular protists are whole, complete, independent organisms that must compete and survive as such in the environments in which they live. Adaptations to particular habitats over eons of time have resulted in both intracellular and extracellular elaborations seldom, if ever, found at the cellular level in higher eukaryotic species. Internally, for example, complex rootlet systems have evolved in association with the basal bodies, or kinetosomes, of many ciliates and flagellates, and nonhomologous (i.e., unrelated by a shared ancestry) endoskeletal and exoskeletal structures have developed in many protist taxa. Conspicuous food-storage bodies are often present, and pigment bodies apart from, or in addition to, chloroplasts are found in some species. In the cortex, just under the pellicle (cell covering) of some protists, extrusible bodies (extrusomes) of various types (e.g., trichocysts, haptocysts, toxi-

RESEARCH ON EUKARYOTIC CELL DEVELOPMENT

American biologist Lynn Margulis (1938–2011) developed the serial endosymbiotic theory of eukaryotic cell development, which revolutionized the modern concept of how life arose on Earth.

Throughout most of her career, Margulis was considered a radical by peers who pursued traditional Darwinian "survival of the fittest" approaches to biology. Her ideas, which focused on symbiosis—a living arrangement of two different organisms in an association that can be either beneficial or unfavourable—were frequently greeted with skepticism and even hostility. Among her most important work was the development of the serial endosymbiotic theory (SET) of the origin of cells, which posits that eukaryotic cells (cells with nuclei) evolved from the symbiotic merger of nonnucleated bacteria that had previously existed independently. In this theory, mitochondria and chloroplasts, two major organelles of eukaryotic cells, are descendants of once free-living bacterial species. She explained the concept in her first book, *Origin of Eukaryotic Cells* (1970). At the time, her theory was regarded as far-fetched, but it has since been widely accepted. She elaborated in her 1981 classic, *Symbiosis in Cell Evolution*, proposing that another symbiotic merger of cells with bacteria—this time spirochetes, a type of bacterium that undulates rapidly—developed into

(continued on the next page)

Lynn Margulis's research explained the inner workings of eukaryotic cells and helped lead to new concepts of how life originated.

(continued from the previous page)

the internal transportation system of the nucleated cell. Margulis further postulated that eukaryotic cilia were also originally spirochetes and that cytoplasm evolved from a symbiotic relationship between eubacteria and archaebacteria.

Her 1982 book *Five Kingdoms*, written with American biologist Karlene V. Schwartz, articulates a five-kingdom system of classifying life on Earth—animals, plants, bacteria (prokaryotes), fungi, and protoctists. The protista kingdom, which comprises most unicellular organisms (and multicellular algaes) in other systems, is rejected as too general. Many of the organisms usually categorized as protista are placed in one of the other four kingdoms; protoctists make up the remaining organisms, which are all aquatic, and include algaes and slime molds. Margulis edited portions of the compendium *Handbook of Protoctista* (1990).

cysts, and mucocysts) have evolved, with presumably nonhomologous functions, some of which are still unknown. Scales may appear on the outside of the body, and, in some groups, tentacles, suckers, hooks, spines, hairs, or other anchoring devices have evolved. Many species have an external covering sheath, which is a glycopolysaccharide surface coat sometimes known as the glycocalyx. Cyst or spore walls, stalks, loricae, and shells (or tests) are also common external features.

FORM AND FUNCTION

As a group, the protists consist of many unrelated or loosely related organisms. Thus, there exists enormous diversity in structure and form between them. Some possess a simple oval cell, whereas others have a cell that is surrounded by a wall of armour with a complicated pattern. Some possess simple flagella, whereas others have a single flagella surrounded by a delicate circular collar of fine pseudopodia on which they trap food particles. Furthermore, whereas some contain pigments, others do not. All these variations in structure and biochemical properties ultimately influence how an organism functions. As a result, with the many differences in form, come many differences in function.

LOCOMOTION

One of the most striking features of many protist species is the presence of some type of locomotory organelle, easily visible under the light microscope. A few forms can move by gliding or floating, although the vast majority move by means of "whips" or small "hairs" known as flagella or cilia, respectively. (These organelles give their names to informal groups—flagellates and ciliates—of protists.) A lesser number of protists employ pseudopodia. These same organelles may be used in feeding as well.

Cilia and flagella are basically identical in structure and perhaps fundamentally in function as well. They are far more complex at the molecular level than they may seem to be when viewed solely by light microscopy. Cilia and flagella are also known among plants and animals, although they are totally absent from the true fungi. These eukaryotic organelles are not to be confused with the locomotory structure of bacteria (the prokaryotic flagellum), which is a minute organelle composed of flagellin, not tubulin, as in

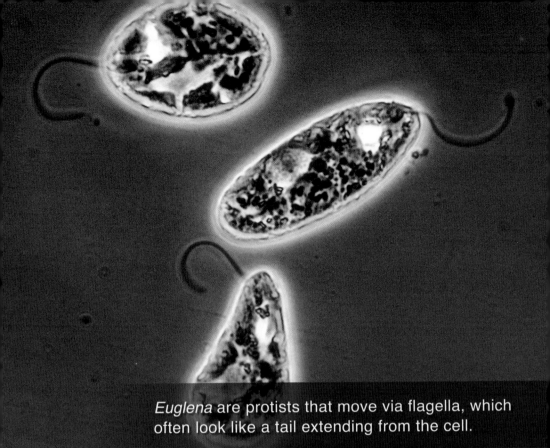

Euglena are protists that move via flagella, which often look like a tail extending from the cell.

the protists. The prokaryotic flagellum is intrinsically nonmotile (rather, it is moved by its basal part, which is embedded in the cell membrane). It is entirely extracellular, and it is neither homologous with (i.e., does not have a common evolutionary origin) nor ancestral to the eukaryotic flagella.

Cilia and flagella consist of an inner cylindrical body known as the axoneme and an outer surrounding membrane, the latter continuous with the cell membrane. The axoneme itself is composed of nine outer pairs of longitudinal microtubules (microtubular fibres) and one inner pair. The nine outer pairs become triplets of microtubules below the surface of the cell. This structure, presumably anchoring the flagellum to the organism's body, is known as the basal body or kinetosome. The membrane of the cilium or flagellum may appear to bear minute scales or hairs (mastigonemes) on its own outer surface, presumably functionally important to the organism and valuable as taxonomic characters. A fibrillar structure within the flagella, known as a paraflagellar, paraxial, or intraflagellar rod, may lie between the axoneme and the outer membrane of a flagellum; its function is not clear.

The distribution of these locomotory organelles over the cell varies among different taxonomic groups. Many of the algal protists characteristically have two flagella, and in most instances both flagella originate near or at the anterior pole of the body. The presence, absence, or pattern of the mastigonemes may also differ between two flagella of the same species and among species belonging to separate taxa. Some of the parasitic zooflagellates have hundreds of long flagella, and the locomotion of some of these species is further aided by the presence of attached spirochetes (prokaryotes) undulating among the flagella.

Ciliated protists show an even greater diversity in the number, distribution, and arrangement of cilia over the cell. In some groups, single cilia have, in effect, been replaced by compound ciliary organelles (e.g., membranelles and cirri), which may be used effectively in locomotion and in feeding. Patterns are again associated with members of different taxa. While both ciliates and flagellates may have various rootlet systems associated with their locomotory organelles or with the basal bodies, or both, the organelles in the ciliates have developed a more complex and elaborate subpellicular infrastructure. Called the infraciliature, or kinetidal system, it lies principally in the outer, or cortical, layer of the ciliate's body (only the outermost layer is called the pellicle) and serves primarily as a skeletal system for the organism. The system is composed of an array of single or paired kinetosomes with associated microtubules and microfibrils plus other specialized organelles (such as parasomal sacs, alveoli, contractile vacuole pores, and the cytoproct, or cell anus), which is unique among the protists. Variations are of great importance in the taxonomy and evolution of protists.

Typically, flagellates move through an aqueous medium by the undulatory motions of the flagella. The waves of movement are generated at the base of the flagellum. The direction and speed of propulsion and other elements of movement depend on a number of factors, including the viscosity of the medium, the size of the organism, the amplitude and length of the waves, the length and exact position of the flagella, and the kind and presence or absence of flagellar hairs. Some ciliates can move much more rapidly by virtue of having many though shorter, cilia beating in coordination with each other. The synchronized beat along the longitudinal ciliary rows produces what is known as a metachronal wave. Differences in details attest to the complexity of the overall process.

Flagella and cilia are also involved in sensory functioning, probably by means of their outer membranes which are known to contain, at the molecular level, as many as seven kinds of receptors. A variety of chemoreceptors can recognize minute changes in the medium surrounding the organism as well as cues from presumed mating partners that lead to sexual behaviour.

In comparison with flagella and cilia, pseudopodia seem rather simple. Pseudopodia are responsible for amoeboid movement. Such movement, however, is not exclusive to the amoebas; some flagellates, some sporozoa (apicomplexans), and even some cells of the other eukaryotic kingdoms demonstrate it. Pseudopodia, even more so than flagella and cilia, are widely used in phagotrophic feeding as well as in locomotion. Three kinds of pseudopods (lobopodia, filopodia, and reticulopodia) are basically similar and are quite widespread among the amoebae, while the fourth type (axopodia) is totally different, more complex, and characteristic of certain specialized phagocytic cells. The types, numbers, shapes, distribution, and actions of pseudopodia are important for distinguishing between the different types of protists.

The lobopodium may be flattened or cylindrical (tubular). *Amoeba proteus* is probably the best-known protist possessing lobose pseudopodia. Although the mechanisms of amoeboid movement have long been a controversial topic, there is general agreement that contraction of the outer, nongranular layer of cytoplasm (the ectoplasm) causes the forward flow of the inner, granular layer of cytoplasm (the endoplasm) into the tip of a pseudopod, thus advancing the whole body of the organism. Actin and myosin microfilaments, adenosine triphosphate (ATP), calcium ions, and other factors are involved in various stages of this complex process.

Other pseudopodia found among the rhizopod amoebas include the filopodia and the reticulopodia. The filopodia are hyaline, slender, and often branching structures in which contraction of microfilaments moves the organism's body along the substrate, even if it is bearing a relatively heavy test or shell. Reticulopodia are fine threads that may not only branch but also anastomose to form a dense network, which is particularly useful in entrapping prey. Microtubules are involved in the mechanism of movement, and the continued migration of an entire reticulum carries the cell in the same direction. The testaceous, or shell-bearing, amoebas possess either lobopodia or filopodia, and the often economically important foraminiferans bear reticulopodia.

The actinopod amoebae are characterized in large measure by the axopodium, the fourth and most distinct type of pseudopodium. Axopodia are composed of an outer layer of flowing cytoplasm that surrounds a central core containing a bundle of microtubules, which are cross-linked in specific patterns among different species. The outer cytoplasm may bear extrusible organelles used in capturing prey. Retraction of an axopod is quite rapid in some forms, although not in others; reextension is generally slow in all actinopods. The modes of movement of the axopodia often differ. For example, the marine pelagic protozoan *Sticholonche* has axopodia that move like oars, even rotating in basal sockets reminiscent of oarlocks.

RESPIRATION AND NUTRITION

At the cellular level, the metabolic pathways known for protists are essentially no different from those found among cells and tissues of other eukaryotes. Thus, the plastids of algal protists function like the chloroplasts of plants with respect to photosynthesis, and, when present, the mitochondria function as the site where molecules are broken down to release chemical energy, carbon dioxide, and water. The basic difference between the unicellular protists and the tissue and organ-dependent cells of other eukaryotes lies in the fact that the former are simultaneously cells and complete organisms. Such microorganisms, then, must carry out the life-sustaining functions that are generally served by organ systems within the complex multicellular or multitissued bodies of the other eukaryotes. Many such functions in the protists are dependent on relatively elaborate architectural adaptations in the cell. Phagotrophic feeding, for example, requires more complicated processes at the protist's cellular level, where no combination of tissues and cells is available to carry out the ingestion, digestion, and egestion of particulate food matter. On the other hand, obtaining oxygen in the case of free-living, free-swimming protozoan protists is simpler than for multicellular eukaryotes because the process requires only the direct diffusion of oxygen from the surrounding medium.

Although most protists require oxygen (obligate aerobes), there are two main groups that may or must exhibit anaerobic metabolism: parasitic forms inhabiting sites without free oxygen and some bottom-dwelling (benthic) ciliates that live in the sulfide zone of certain marine and freshwater sediments. Mitochondria are not found in the cytoplasm of these anaerobes; rather, microbodies called hydrogenosomes or specialized symbiotic bacteria act as respiratory organelles.

The major modes of nutrition are autotrophy (involving plastids, photosynthesis, and the organism's manufacture of its own nutrients from the milieu) and heterotrophy (the taking in of nutrients). Obligate autotrophy, which requires only a few inorganic materials and light energy for survival and growth, is characteristic of algal protists (e.g., *Chlamydomonas*).

Heterotrophy may occur as one of at least two types: phagotrophy, which is essentially the engulfment of particulate food, and osmotrophy, the taking in of dissolved nutrients from the medium, often by the method of pinocytosis. Phagotrophic heterotrophy is seen in many ciliates that seem to require live prey as organic sources of energy, carbon, nitrogen, vitamins, and growth factors. The food of free-living phagotrophic protists ranges from other protists to bacteria to plant and animal material, living or dead. Scavengers are numerous, especially among the ciliophorans. Indeed, species of some groups prefer moribund prey. Organisms that can utilize either or both autotrophy and heterotrophy are said to exhibit mixotrophy. Many dinoflagellates, for example, exhibit mixotrophy, one of the reasons they are claimed taxonomically by both botanists and zoologists.

Feeding mechanisms and their use are diverse among protists. They include the capture of living prey by the use of encircling pseudopodial extensions (in certain rhizopods), the trapping of particles of food in water currents by filters formed of specialized compound buccal organelles (in ciliates), and the simple diffusion of dissolved organic material through the cell membrane, as well as the sucking out of the cytoplasm of certain host cells (as in many parasitic protists). In the case of many symbiotic protists, methods for survival, such as the invasion of the host and transfer to fresh hosts, have developed through long associations and often the coevolution of both partners.

REPRODUCTION AND LIFE CYCLES

Cell division in protists, as in plant and animal cells, is not a simple process, although it may superficially appear to be so. A common mode of protist reproduction is asexual binary fission. The body of an individual protist is simply pinched into two parts or halves. The "parental" body disappears and is replaced by a pair of offspring or daughter nuclei, although the latter may need to mature somewhat to be recognizable as members of the parental species. The length of time for completion of the process of binary fission varies among groups of organisms and with environmental conditions, but it may be said to range from just a few hours in an optimal situation to many days under other circumstances. In some unicellular algal protists, reproduction occurs by fragmentation. Mitotic replications of the nuclear material presumably accompany or precede all divisions of the cytoplasm (cytokinesis) in protists.

Multiple fission also occurs among protists and is common in some parasitic species. The nucleus divides repeatedly to produce a number of daughter nuclei, which eventually become the nuclei of the progeny after repeated cellular divisions. There are several kinds of multiple fission, often correlated with phases or stages in the full life cycle of a given species. The number of offspring or filial products resulting from a multiple division (or very rapid succession of binary fissions) may vary from four to dozens or even hundreds, generally in a short period of time. Modes of such multiple fission range from budding, in which a daughter nucleus is produced and split from the parent together with some of the surrounding cytoplasm, to sporogony (production of sporozoites by repeated divisions of a zygote) and schizogony (formation of multiple merozoites, as in malarial parasites). The latter two phenomena are characteristic of many sporozoan protists, which are obligate parasites of more advanced eukaryotes. Some multicellular algal protists reproduce via asexual spores, structures that are themselves often produced by a series of rapid fissions.

Even under a light microscope, differences can be seen in the modes of division among diverse groups of protists. The flagellates, for example, exhibit a longitudinal, or mirror-image, type of fission (symmetrogeny). The ciliates, on the other hand, basically divide in a point-by-point correspondence of parts (homothetogeny), often seen as essentially transverse or perkinetal (across the kineties, or ciliary rows). In general, most amoebas exhibit, in effect, no clear-cut body symmetry or polarity, and thus their fission is basically simpler and falls into neither of the categories described above.

Sexual phenomena are known among the protists. The erroneous view that practically all protists reproduce asexually is explained by the fact that certain well-known organisms, such as species belonging to the genera *Euglena* and *Amoeba*, do not demonstrate sexuality. Even many of the unicellular species can, under appropriate conditions, form gametes (male and female sex cells, although sometimes multiple sexes are formed, which makes the terms *male* and *female* inappropriate), which fuse and give rise to a new generation. In fact, sexual reproduction— the union of one male and one female gamete (syngamy, or fertilization)—is the most common sexual phenomenon and occurs quite widely among the protists—for example, among algae, among various flagellate and amoeboid groups, and among many parasitic phyla (e.g., in *Plasmodium*, the genus of malaria-causing organisms).

Conjugation, the second major kind of sexual phenomenon and one occurring in the ciliated protists, has genetic and evolutionary results identical to those of syngamy. The process involves the fusion of gametic nuclei rather than independent gamete cells. Azygotic, or fusion, nucleus (not a true zygote) is produced and undergoes a series of meiotic divisions to produce a number of haploid pronuclei. All but one of these pronuclei in each organism will disintegrate. The remaining pronuclei divide mitotically. One pronucleus from each organism is exchanged, and the new micronuclei and macronuclei of the next generation are formed. Following the exchange of the pronuclei and the subsequent formation of new micronuclei and macronuclei in each organism, a series of asexual fissions, accompanied by mitotic divisions of the new diploid micronuclei, occurs in each exconjugant line. The new polyploid macronuclei are distributed passively in the first of these divisions. In subsequent fission, the macronuclei duplicate themselves through a form of mitosis. This last stage constitutes the only reproduction involved in the process.

Conjugation is essentially limited to the ciliates and certain algae, and there is considerable variation in the manner in which it is exhibited among them. For example, the two ciliates themselves may be of noticeably different size (called macroconjugants and microconjugants), or the number of predivisions of the micronuclei may vary, as may the number of nuclear divisions that take place after the zygotic nucleus is formed. Furthermore, chemical signals (gamones) are given or exchanged before a pair of protists unite in conjugation. It is not known if these gamones should be considered as sex pheromones, reminiscent of those known in many animals (for example, certain insects), but they seem to serve the similar purpose of attracting or bringing together different mating types.

While conjugation may be considered a process of reciprocal fertilization, a parallel sexual phenomenon in ciliates, which takes place in single, unpaired individuals, may be considered a process of self-fertilization. In this type of fertilization, called autogamy, complete homozygosity is obtained in the lines derived from the single parent, and the species that seem to prefer this process are known as intensive inbreeders.

Protist life cycles range from relatively simple ones that may involve only periodic binary fissions to very complex schemes that may contain asexual and sexual phases, encystment and excystment, and—in the case of many symbiotic and parasitic forms—an alternation of hosts. In the more complicated life cycles in particular, the morphology of the organism may be strikingly different (polymorphism) from phase to phase in the entire life cycle. Among certain ciliate groups in which a larval or migratory form (known as a swarmer) is produced by the parent, the offspring may demonstrate such a differing morphology that it might well be assigned taxonomically to an entirely different family, order, or even class.

Dormant stages in a life cycle are probably more common in algal protists than in protozoan protists. Such stages, somewhat analogous to hibernation in mammals, serve to preserve the species during unfavourable conditions, as in times of inadequate food supply or extreme temperatures. The occurrence of resistant cysts in the vegetative stage depends, therefore, on such environmental factors as season, temperature, light, water, and nutrient supply. The fertilized egg, or zygote, in a number of algal groups may also pass into a dormant stage (a zygospore). Temporary or long-lasting cysts may occur among other protist species as well. Many sporozoa and members of other totally parasitic phyla form a highly resistant stage—for example, the oocyst of the coccidians, which may survive for a long time in the fecal material of the host or in the soil. This cyst is the infective stage for the next host in the parasite's life cycle.

Some life cycles involve not only multiple hosts but also a vector—that is, a particular metazoan organism that can act as either an active or a passive carrier of the parasite to the next host. In malaria, for example, a mosquito is required to transfer the *Plasmodium* species to the next vertebrate host.

ECOLOGY

The distribution of protists is worldwide. As a group, these organisms are both cosmopolitan and ubiquitous. Every individual species, however, has preferred niches and microhabitats, and all protists are to some degree sensitive to changes in their surroundings. The availability of sufficient nutrients and water, as well as sunlight for photosynthetic forms, is, however, the only major factor restraining successful and heavy protist colonization of practically any habitat on Earth.

Free-living forms are particularly abundant in natural aquatic systems, such as ponds, streams, rivers, lakes, bays, seas, and oceans. Certain of these forms may occur at specific levels in the water column, or they may be bottom-dwellers (benthic). More specialized, sometimes human-made, habitats are also often well populated by both pigmented and nonpigmented protists. Such sites include thermal springs, briny pools, cave waters, snow and ice, beach sands and intertidal mud flats, bogs and marshes, swimming pools, and sewage treatment plants. Many are commonly found in various terrestrial habitats, such as soils, forest litter, desert sands, and the bark and leaves of trees. Cysts and spores may be recovered from considerable heights in the atmosphere, and some researchers claim that certain algal protists actually live, and perhaps reproduce, in air streams.

This foraminifera fossil, found on a beach in the Maldives, is about 1 mm (0.04 inch) wide and magnified through a scanning electron micrograph.

Fossilized forms are plentiful in the geologic record. They are found in strata of all ages, as far back, in the case of red alga fossils, as 1.9 billion years ago. Entire groups of protists have left no record of their now extinct forms, making speculation about early phylogenetic and evolutionary relationships difficult to verify with the types of hard data available in the study of animal and plant evolution. Symbiotic protists are as widespread as free-living forms, since they occur everywhere their hosts are to be found. Hundreds or even thousands of kinds of protists live as ectosymbionts or episymbionts, finding suitable niches with plants, fungi, vertebrate and invertebrate animals, or even other protists. Seldom are the hosts harmed. In fact, these often mobile substrates are actually used as a means of dispersal.

Endosymbionts include commensals, facultative parasites, and obligate parasites. The latter category embraces forms that have effects on their hosts ranging from mild discomfort to death. Protozoan and certainly nonphotosynthetic protists are implicated far more often in such associations than are algal forms. In a few protists, both cytoplasm and nuclei can be invaded by other protists, and intimate, mutually beneficial relationships between protistan hosts and protistan symbionts have been seen, such as foraminiferans or ciliates that nourish symbiotic algae in their cytoplasm. When higher eukaryotes are hosts to protists, all body cavities and organ systems are susceptible to invasion, although terrestrial plants bear relatively few such parasites. In animal hosts, the principal areas serving as sites for endosymbiotic species are the digestive tract and its associated organs and the circulatory system.

The numbers of individuals in populations of many protists reach staggering figures. There are, on the average, tens of thousands of protists in a gram of arable soil, hundreds of thousands in the gut of a termite, millions in the rumen of a bovine mammal, billions in a tiny patch of floating plankton in the sea, and trillions in the bloodstream of a person infected

Researchers at Westminster University in London have developed a genetically altered fungus that can attack the protozoans that cause malaria.

with severe malaria. Fossil forms reach similar, if not greater, concentrations.

Some of the most severe diseases of humans are caused by protists, primarily blood parasites. Malaria (caused by protozoans of genus *Plasmodium*), the various trypanosomiases (caused by flagellated protozoans of genus *Trypanosoma*) and leishmaniasis (caused by tissue-invading flagellates of genus *Leishmania*), toxoplasmosis (caused by prototozoans in genus *Toxoplasma*), and amoebic dysentery (caused by the protozoan *Entamoeba histolytica*) are debilitating or fatal afflictions. Biomedical research still needs to be carried out to find ways of controlling and eradicating such diseases of humans.

Protist parasites infecting domesticated livestock, poultry, hatchery fishes, and other such food sources deplete supplies or render them unpalatable. The economic losses can be considerable. Certain free-living marine dinoflagellates are the causative agents of the so-called red tide outbreaks that occur periodically along coasts throughout the world. A toxin released by the blooming protists kills fishes in the area by the hundreds of tons. Other dinoflagellates produce a toxin that may be taken up by certain shellfish (bivalve mollusks) and which causes paralysis, even death, when the mollusk is eaten by humans.

Many protists provide humans with benefits, some more obvious than others. Because many protists (e.g., planktonic algae) are located at or near the bottom of the food chain in nature, they serve a crucial role in sustaining the higher eukaryotes in fresh and marine waters. In addition to directly and indirectly supplying organic molecules (such as sugars) for other organisms, the pigmented (chlorophyll-containing) algal protists produce oxygen as a by-product of photosynthesis. Algae may supply up to half of the net global oxygen. Deposits of natural gas and crude oil are derived from fossilized populations of algal protists. Much of the nutrient turnover and mineral recycling in the oceans and seas comes from the activities of the hetero-trophic (nonpigmented) flagellates and the ciliates living there, species that feed on the bacteria and other primary protists present in the same milieu. Seaweeds (e.g., brown algae) have long been used as fertilizers. Several hundred species of algae are consumed as food, either directly or indirectly in prepared items. For example, alginates (extracted from brown algae) and agars (from red algae) occur in foods such as ice cream, candy bars, puddings, and pie fillings. The calcareous test, or shell, of the foraminiferans is preservable and constitutes a major component of limestone rocks. Assemblages of cer-tain of these protists, which are abundant and usually easily recognized, are known to have been deposited during various specific periods in the Earth's geologic history. Geologists in the petroleum industry study for-aminiferan species present in samples of drilled cores in order to determine the age of different strata in the Earth's crust, thus making possible the identification of rich oil deposits. Before synthetic substitutes, black-board chalk consisted mostly of calcium carbonate derived from the scales (coccoliths) of certain algal protists and from the tests of foraminiferans. Diatoms and some ciliate species are useful as indicators of water quality and therefore of the amount of pollution in natural aquatic systems and in sewage purification plants. Selected species of parasitic protozoans may play a significant role as biological control organisms against certain insect predators of food plants.

Protists have been used as model cells in laboratory research, some of which is directed against major human diseases. The combination of characteristics that has made them superior to both prokaryotic cells and other eukaryotic cells includes their easy availability and maintenance, convenient size for handling in large numbers, short generation time, broad physiological adaptability, basic structural and functional similarity to the eukaryotic cells of animal organisms, and, most importantly for sophisticated work requiring purity of material and rigidity of controls, culturability (i.e., their successful growth axenically—free of other living organisms—and on chemically definable media). The culturability of some unicellular free-living protists has made them invaluable as assay organisms and pharmacological tools. Among those that have proven to be useful this way, the most important is the ciliate *Tetrahymena*, which serves as a superb model cell in investigations in cell and molecular biology. The value of such research in such biomedically important fields as cancer chemotherapy is potentially great.

EVOLUTION AND PALEOPROTISTOLOGY

Students of the evolution of most lines of plants and animals have relied heavily on the fossil records of their forms to indicate ancestor-descendant relationships over time. In the case of most protist groups, extinct forms are rare or too scattered to be of much help in evolutionary studies. For certain major groups, fossil forms are abundant, and such material is useful in an investigation of their probable interrelationships, but only at lower taxonomic levels within those groups themselves. Speculation about the possible degrees of phylogenetic closeness (or relatedness of evolutionary histories) among the various protists is frustrated by the lack of appropriate fossil material. There are other ways and means of determining relationships, but these are also only partially helpful. The application of modern techniques of sequencing proteins and genes to problems of evolutionary protistology is offering invaluable assistance in these investigations.

Paleoprotistology, the study of extinct protists (i.e., of the protists that were capable of becoming fossilized: cell, cyst, or spore walls; internal or external skeletons of appropriate preservable materials; and scales, loricae, tests, or shells) has thrown light on the probable interrelationships of both fossil and contemporary forms within classes, orders, and genera and on the paleoecology of the geologic eras and periods in which the fossil forms once lived. In addition, it has provided valuable information on the antiquity of the groups being examined. Caution is necessary, however, since species with no hard parts left no fossil record, and the extinct forms that are studied may have been preceded by species that have left specimens not yet discovered.

The antiquity of several major groups of protists, however, has been quite well established. The rhodophytes (red algae) may have arisen as early as 1.9 billion years ago, during the Proterozoic Eon, although most of their fossils are from more recent geologic periods. The polycystine actinopods (classically known as the radiolarians) and various green algal protist lines also have origins in this period. Foraminiferans, dinoflagellates, haptophytes (a group of algae), and some brown algae (phaeophytes) date to the middle of the Paleozoic Era (some 300 to 400 million years ago).

Representatives of a number of protist taxa (including the ubiquitous diatoms) have been found as fossils from protists of the Mesozoic Era (100 to 200 million years ago). A useful method of tackling the broad problems of possible phylogenetic interrelationships among diverse high-level protist groups is the recognition of homologous (or presumed homologous) structures within representative forms. Electron microscopy has been important in comparative studies of this kind. Ultrastructural characteristics exhibited in common by groups seemingly as diverse as green euglenoid protists and the parasitic trypanosome "zooflagellates," for example, caused major changes in the systematics of protists. The principal features of high phylogenetic-information content are the microfibrillar and microtubular organelles associated with the basal bodies (kinetosomes) of all flagellated and ciliated protists; the mastigonemes, or flagellar "hairs," found on many flagella, especially of algal protists; the configuration of the cristae formed by the infolding of the inner membrane of mitochondria; the characteristics of plastids, including the number of surrounding membranes or envelopes; microtubular cytoskeletal systems not directly associated with cilia and flagella; extrusomes; and cell walls and walls and membranes of various spores, cysts, tests, and loricae.

Biochemical and physiological characteristics, sometimes directly related functionally to the anatomic ultrastructures mentioned above, include the exact nature of the pigments in those protists with plastids, of the storage products produced (food reserves), and of the cell walls or membranes enveloping the organism. Determination of the molecular structure or functions of cytoplasmic inclusions, such as mitochondria, the Golgi apparatus, lysosomes, microbodies of diverse sorts, pseudopodia, spindle fibres (which function in mitosis and meiosis), and even miscellaneous vesicles, vacuoles, and membranes, can throw light on group affinities. Comparing metabolic pathways can be valuable as well. For example, the choice of lysine biosynthesis differs among various protist groups. Modes of nutrition are also investigated.

General ecological factors or characteristics have not played an important role in these studies. Specifically implicated in hypotheses of the origin of eukaryotic cells from prokaryotic ancestries (eukaryogenesis), however, is the phenomenon of endosymbiosis, which in a broad sense might be considered an ecological factor in the very early evolution of organisms destined to comprise the eukaryotic kingdoms. The serial endosymbiosis theory (or SET), first described by American biologist Lynn Margulis in her book *Origin of Eukaryotic Cells* (1970), offers one explanation of the origin of such cytoplasmic organelles as the mitochondria and plastids found in so many protists. According to SET, certain primitive prokaryotes were engulfed by other, different prokaryotes. The structures and functions of the first were ultimately incorporated into the second. The second form—now more highly evolved and presumably favoured by selection—could subsequently engulf, or be invaded by, still other types of primitive prokaryotes, acquiring from them additional, and different, structures and functions. Through its own internal evolution as well, this more complex organism eventually came to possess the characteristics recognizable as eukaryotic. This exogenous theory is to be contrasted with the endogenous hypothesis, which has held that all cellular organelles have been derived, in a long evolutionary process, from materials (especially membranes) already present in the (potential) eukaryotic cell.

Ribosomal RNA sequencing is a molecular technique that has had a major impact on conventional schemes of classification of the protists. It has, however, also strengthened or confirmed older systems that were based either on intuitive deductions or on the determination of ultrastructural homologies. The protists are thought to have arisen from bacteria (not archaea), with symbiotic associations being involved in some way. The first, or "eoprotist," was probably a nonpigmented heterotrophic form. From within the vast array of protists there must have arisen the early members of the other eukaryotic kingdoms, as well as still additional protist groups. Numerous groups undoubtedly arose as evolutionary experiments, and many of these subsequently became extinct, generally leaving no fossil record. The protists are themselves likely someday to be subdivided into several separate kingdoms.

CHAPTER

5

TYPES OF PROTOZOANS

P rotistan species are predominantly unicellular in organization and microscopic in size. They are eukaryotic organisms possessing, at most, one tissue—tissue being an aggregation of similar cells and their products forming a definite, specialized kind of structural material. The relatively few syncytial (coenocytic), coenobial, or multicellular forms, which generally appear as filaments, colonies, coenobia, or thalli, still do not exhibit a true multi-tissue organization in the active (vegetative) stage. Macroscopic sizes are attained by species of a few groups (notably the brown algae). There are no truly vascular protists. All eukaryotic modes of nutrition exist among the protists, with both phototrophic and heterotrophic types being common. Cysts or spores occur widely. Motility is frequently exhibited, principally via flagella, cilia, or pseudopodia. In general, motility in at least one stage of the life cycle is more common among the protists than are completely nonmotile forms. Both intracellular and extracellular elaborations (such as the organelles and the skeleton) show considerable complexity in protists.

The diversity that exists among the numerous characteristics of the group supports the hypothesis that protists were ancestral to the other three eukaryotic kingdoms. For example, the distribution of the protists is ubiquitous and cosmopolitan. They show all modes of nutrition, and some species may exhibit only aerobic respiration and others only anaerobic respiration. In aerobic groups, the mitochondrial cristae are tubular, vesicular, lamellar (flattened), or discoidal, and mitotic and meiotic mechanisms and types are diverse. The total number of acceptably described species, extinct and extant, may be estimated to reach at least 120,000, with another 80,000 (mostly fossil forms) on record but of questionable validity.

Protozoans are organisms that are usually single-celled and heterotrophic (using organic carbon as a source of energy) belonging to any of the major lineages of protists and, like most protists, typically microscopic. Modern science has shown that the protozoans represent a very complicated grouping of organisms that do not necessarily share a common evolutionary history. This unrelated, or paraphyletic, nature of the protozoans has caused scientists to abandon the term *protozoan* in formal classification schemes. Hence, the subkingdom Protozoa is now considered obsolete. Today the term *protozoan* is used informally in reference to nonfilamentous heterotrophic protists. Commonly known protozoans include representative dinoflagellates, amoebas, paramecia, and the malaria-causing *Plasmodium*. Although protozoans are no longer recognized as

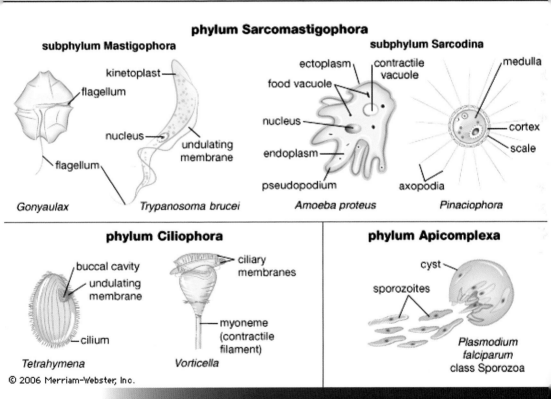

Protozoans are diverse in structure and many other features. Members of the subphylum Sarcodina usually possess protective coverings; the heliozoan Pinaciophora is shown covered with scales. The phylum Ciliophora contains the greatest number of protozoan species but is the most homogeneous group.

a formal group in current biological classification systems, *protozoan* can still be useful as a strictly descriptive term.

CLASSIFICATION PROBLEMS

When microscopy arose as a science in its own right, botanists and zoologists discovered evidence of the vast diversity of life mostly invisible to the unaided eye. With rare exception, authorities of the time classified such microscopic forms as minute plants (called algae) and minute animals (called "first animals," or protozoa). Such taxonomic assignments went essentially unchallenged for many years, despite the fact that the great majority of those minute forms of life—not to mention certain macroscopic ones, various parasitic forms, and the entire group known as the fungi—did not possess the cardinal characteristics on which the "plants" and "animals" had been differentiated and thus had to be forced to fit into those kingdom categories.

In 1860, however, British naturalist John Hogg took exception to the imposition of the plant and animal categories on the protists and proposed a fourth kingdom, named Protoctista (the other three kingdoms encompassed the animals, the plants, and the minerals). Six years later German zoologist Ernst Haeckel (having dropped the mineral kingdom) proposed a third kingdom, the Protista, to embrace microorganisms. In the late 1930s American botanist Herbert F. Copeland proposed a separate kingdom for the bacteria (kingdom Monera), based on their unique absence of a clearly defined nucleus. Under Copeland's arrangement, the kingdom Protista thus consisted of nucleated life that was neither plant nor animal. The following decade he revived the name Protoctista, using it in favour of Protista.

The next major change in the systematics of lower forms came through an advancement in the concept of the composition of the biotic world. About 1960, resurrecting and embellishing an idea originally conceived two decades earlier by French marine biologist Edouard Chatton but universally overlooked, Roger Yate Stanier, Cornelius B. van Niel, and their colleagues formally proposed the division of all living things into two great groups, the prokaryotes and the eukaryotes. This organization was based on characteristics—such as the presence or absence of a true nucleus, the simplicity or complexity of the DNA (deoxyribonucleic acid) molecules constituting the chromosomes, and the presence or absence of intracellular membranes (and of specialized organelles apart from ribosomes) in the cytoplasm—that revealed a long phylogenetic separation of the two assemblages. The concept of "protists" originally embraced all the microorganisms in the biotic world. The entire assemblage thus included the protists plus the bacteria, the latter considered at that time to be lower protists. The great evolutionary boundary between the prokaryotes and the eukaryotes, however, has meant a major taxonomic boundary restricting the protists to eukaryotic microorganisms (but occasionally including relatively macroscopic organisms) and the bacteria to prokaryotic microorganisms.

During the 1970s and '80s, attention was redirected to the problem of possible high-level systematic subdivisions within the eukaryotes. American biologists Robert H. Whittaker and Lynn Margulis, as well as others, became involved in such challenging questions. A major outcome was widespread support among botanists and zoologists for considering living organisms as constituting five separate kingdoms, four of which were placed in what was conceived of as the superkingdom Eukaryota (Protista, Plantae, Animalia, and Fungi); the fifth kingdom, Monera, constituted the superkingdom Prokaryota.

In the late 1970s, realizing distinctions between certain prokaryotes, American microbiologist Carl R. Woese proposed a system whereby life was divided into three domains: Eukarya for all eukaryotes, Bacteria for the true bacteria, and Archaea for primitive prokaryotes that are distinct from true bacteria. Woese's scheme was unique for its focus on molecular characteristics, particularly certain RNA sequences. Although imperfect, RNA analyses have provided great insight into the evolutionary relatedness of organisms, which in turn has led to extensive reassessment of protist taxonomy such that many scientists no longer consider kingdom Protista to be a valid grouping.

SELECT GROUPS OF PROTOZOANS

In order to more clearly understand the form and function of protists, it is simplest to begin with an examination of the most common and best-characterized organisms. Among these are *Amoeba*, *Euglena*, and *Paramecium*. In addition, organisms such as those in the genera *Plasmodium* and *Trypanosoma* are valuable for understanding the role of protists in human disease.

AMOEBA

In general, the term *amoebae* is used to describe microscopic unicellular protozoans that are characterized by the presence of lobose pseudopodia. Amoebas are readily identified by their ability to form temporary pseudopodia, which they utilize as a form of locomotion. This type of movement, called amoeboid movement, is considered to be the most primitive form of animal locomotion. In a narrower sense, the term *amoeba* refers to the genus *Amoeba*. The well-known type species, *Amoeba proteus*, is found on decaying bottom vegetation of freshwater streams and ponds.

There are numerous parasitic amoebas. Of six species found in the human alimentary tract, *Entamoeba histolytica* causes amebic dysentery. Two related freeliving genera of increasing biomedical importance are *Acanthamoeba* and *Naegleria*, strains of which have been recognized as disease-causing parasites in several vertebrates, including humans.

Amoebas are used extensively in cell research for determining the relative functions and interactions of the nucleus and the cytoplasm. Each amoeba contains a small mass of jellylike cytoplasm, which is differentiated into a thin outer plasma membrane, a layer of stiff, clear ectoplasm just within the plasma membrane, and a central granular endoplasm. The endoplasm contains food vacuoles, a granular nucleus, and a clear contractile vacuole. The amoeba has no mouth or anus. Instead, food is taken in and material excreted at any point on the cell surface. During feeding, extensions of cytoplasm flow around food particles, surrounding them and forming a vacuole into which enzymes are secreted to digest the particles. Oxygen diffuses into the cell from the surrounding water, and metabolic wastes diffuse from the amoeba into the surrounding water. A contractile vacuole, which removes excess water from the amoeba, is absent in most marine and parasitic species. Reproduction is asexual (binary fission).

During adverse environmental periods many amoebas survive by encystment: the amoeba

In this image of an amoeba, the pseudopodia (false feet) it uses to move are clearly visible.

becomes circular, loses most of its water, and secretes a cyst membrane that serves as a protective covering. When the environment is again suitable, the envelope ruptures, and the amoeba emerges.

CILIATE

Ciliates are members of the protozoan phylum Ciliophora, of which there are some 8,000 species. They are generally considered the most evolved and complex of protozoans. Ciliates are single-celled organisms that, at some stage in their life cycle, possess cilia, short hairlike organelles used for locomotion and food gathering. The cilia are usually arranged in rows, known as kineties, on the pellicle (cell covering), but they may fuse together near the cytostome (cell mouth) of some species to form membranelles or undulating membranes (various sheetlike or fan-shaped groupings of cilia). Elsewhere on the pellicle, cilia may form limb-like tufts called cirri. Most ciliates have a flexible pellicle and contractile vacuoles, and many contain toxicysts or other trichocysts, small organelles with thread- or thorn-like structures that can be discharged for anchorage, for defense, or for capturing prey.

Ciliates have one or more macronuclei and from one to several micronuclei. The macronuclei control metabolic and developmental functions, whereas the micronuclei are necessary for reproduction. Reproduction is typically asexual, although sexual exchange occurs as well. Asexual replication is usually by transverse binary fission or by budding. Sexual phenomena include conjugation (genetic exchange between individuals) and autogamy (nuclear reorganization within an individual). Sexual reproduction does not always result in an immediate increase in numbers. However, conjugation is often followed by binary fission. Although most ciliates are free-living and aquatic, such as the *Paramecium*, many are ectocommensals, dwelling harmlessly on the gills or integument of inverte-brates, and some, such as the dysentery-causing *Balantidium*, are parasitic.

EUGLENA

Euglena is a genus of single-celled organisms with both plant and animal characteristics. It is consid-ered a member of the protozoan phylum Eugleno-zoa. The genus is characterized by an elongated cell (15 to 500 micrometres, or 0.0006 to 0.02 inch) with one nucleus, mostly with pigment-containing chloroplasts (although some species are colour-less), a contractile vacuole, an eyespot (stigma), and flagella. Certain species (e.g., *E. rubra*) appear red in sunlight because they contain a large amount of carotenoid pigment.

Some species, which lack a rigid cellulose wall, have a flexible pellicle that allows changes in shape. Food, absorbed directly through the cell surface or produced by photosynthesis, is stored as a complex carbohydrate (paramylum). Reproduction is asex-ual, by longitudinal cell division; sexual reproduction is unknown. Species of *Euglena* live in fresh and brackish water rich in organic matter. Some species develop large populations as green or red "blooms" in ponds or lakes. Several species produce resting cysts that can withstand drying. The colourless spe-cies, including some called *Astasia*, can be used to study cell growth and metabolism in various environmental conditions.

FLAGELLATE

Protozoan flagellates are any of a group of mostly uninucleate organisms, that possess, at some time in the life cycle, one to many flagella for locomotion and sensation. Many flagellates have a thin, firm pellicle or a coating of a jellylike substance. Reproduction is either asexual (usually by longitudinal splitting) or sexual. The protist flagellates are typically placed in subphylum Mastigophora and may be divided taxonomically into two classes, those resembling plants, Phytomastigophorea, and those resembling animals, Zoomastigophorea.

The Phytomastigophorea includes chlorophyll-containing protozoans that can produce their food photosynthetically, as do plants—e.g., *Euglena* and dinoflagellates. Distinctions between phytoflagellates and algae are obscure. Some phytoflagellates are placed with algae in some botanical classifications. Members of the class Zoomastigophorea are colourless, animallike protozoans—e.g., symbiotic hypermastigids. Zooflagellate species in the digestive tracts of termites and roaches enable these insects to utilize the nutrients in cellulose.

Flagellates may be solitary, colonial (*Volvox*), free-living (*Euglena*), or parasitic (the disease-causing

Trypanosoma). Parasitic forms live in the intestine or bloodstream of the host. Many other flagellates (dino-flagellates) live as plankton in both salt and freshwater.

FORAMINIFERAN

Foraminiferans are unicellular organisms character-ized by long, fine pseudopodia that extend from a uninucleated or multinucleated cytoplasmic body encased within a test, or shell. Depending on the species, the test ranges in size from minute to more than 5 cm (2 inches) in diameter and varies in shape, number of chambers, chemical composition, and surface orientation. Tests of a South Pacific species are large enough to be used as jewelry by oceanic islanders. Nummulite specimens from the Eocene limestones of the Egyptian pyramids often exceed 5 cm (2 inches) in diameter. Foraminiferans inhabit virtually all marine waters and are found at almost all depths, wherever there is protection and suitable food (microscopic organisms).

An important constituent of the present-day planktonic (floating) and benthic (bottom-dwelling) microfaunas, foraminiferans have an extensive fos-sil record that makes them useful as index fossils in geological dating and in petroleum exploration. The word foraminiferan does not refer to the exter-nal pores found in some species but to the foramina (openings or apertures) between adjacent chambers after a new chamber envelops a previous one. When the foraminiferans die, their empty calcareous tests sink and form the so-called foraminiferal ooze that covers about 30 percent of the ocean floor. Limestone and chalk are products of the foraminiferan bottom deposits. The major factors governing the growth, reproduction, and distribution of foraminiferans are water temperature, depth, and salinity; availability of suitable food; nature of the substratum; and oxygen supply. The present-day foraminiferan population of the seas consists of six recognizably different faunas. Four of these occur in warmer waters, and two occur in colder waters.

Although some species of foraminiferans reproduce exclusively by asexual means (multiple fission, budding, fragmentation), for most species there is a regular or an occasional sexual generation. Reproduction usually occupies one to three days, depending on the size and complexity of the species. Small species may complete both the sexual and asexual generations within a month, but larger species often require a year or two. Reproduction normally terminates the life of the parent, since all its cytoplasm is generally devoted to formation of the young.

GREGARINE

Gregarines are protozoans that occur as parasites in the body cavities and the digestive systems of invertebrates. Representative genera are *Monocystis* in earthworms and *Gregarina* in locusts and cockroaches. Long and wormlike, gregarines may reach a length of 10 mm (0.4 inch). They often develop in host cells, from which they emerge to reproduce in some body cavity. Feeding by osmosis, some forms attach themselves to a body cavity lining by an anterior hook (epimerite), while others move freely. The gregarines may be divided into three different groups on the basis of the type of life cycle. One group is characterized by a form of asexual reproduction called merogony (nuclear division followed by cytoplasmic division), which precedes sexual union and spore formation. In the second group, merogony is absent, and in the third group merogony occurs in the asexual phase, with each gametocyte producing one spore.

HELIOFLAGELLATE

Helioflagellates are freshwater protozoans that are sometimes considered relatives of the heliozoans (organisms having pseudopodia but no flagella) because of their slender radiating cytoplasmicpseudopodia.

The cores of the pseudopodia of somegenera of helioflagellates radiate from a central granule, as they do in some heliozoans. Helioflagellate life cycles involve alternations between flagellate and heliozoan phases. They reproduce asexually by binary fission. Members of the representative genus *Ciliophrys* are spherical in shape and have a flagellum and very slender pseudopodia. In contrast, those of the genus *Dimorpha* are oval in shape.

HELIOZOAN

Heliozoans are spherical and predominantly fresh-water protozoans that are found either floating or stalked. They are frequently enveloped by a shell (or test) composed of silica or organic material secreted by the organism in the form of scales or pieces in a gelatinous covering. The secretions exhibit a wide variety of shapes, which may help in species identification. The numerous radiating pseudopodia (axopodia) are used more for capturing food than for locomotion. Heliozoans ingest protozoans, algae, and other small organisms and reproduce asexually by binary fission or by budding. Flagellated forms, which may be gametes, have been described in several genera.

Actinophrys sol is a common species often referred to as the sun animalcule. *Acanthocystis turfacea* is a similar species commonly called the green sun animalcule because its body is coloured by harmless symbiotic green algae (zoochlorellae). *Actinosphaerium* species are multinucleate, often reaching a diameter of 1 mm (0.04 inch).

LEISHMANIA

Several species of flagellate protists belong to the genus *Leishmania*. These protists are parasites of vertebrates, to which they are transmitted by species of *Phlebotomus*, a genus of bloodsucking sand flies. The leishmanial parasites assume two forms: a round or oval leishmanial stage, which lives and multiplies in the vertebrate host; and an elongate, motile, flagellated organism called a leptomonad, which is found in the alimentary tract of the sand fly. In their leishmanial stage, the organisms are taken in with the meal of the fly, and they develop into leptomonads in the fly's stomach and multiply there. They eventually migrate to the fly's mouthparts, from which the leptomonads enter the wound made at the next feeding, thus initiating a new infection.

There are three separate species in the genus *Leishmania*: these three species look quite alike but cause three different human diseases that are collectively called leishmaniasis. *L. donovani*, which attacks the liver, spleen, bone marrow, and other viscera, causes kala-azar in Africa, Europe, and Asia. *L. tropica* causes oriental sore in Africa, Europe, and the East; lesions that range from pimples to large ulcers are formed on the skin of the hands, feet, legs, and face. *L. brasiliensis*, the cause of American leishmaniasis in Central and South America, produces similar skin lesions but also causes deeper lesions of the oral and nasal mucous membranes.

MYXOMYCETES

Myxomycetes are fungus-like protists that are commonly known as true slime molds. They exhibit characteristics of both protozoans and fungi. Distributed worldwide, they usually occur in decaying plant material. The vegetative (active, growing, feeding) phase consists of a multinucleate amoeboid mass or sheet (plasmodium). This gives rise to fruiting structures (sporangia) with one to many spores at the head of a stalk. In nearly all species, spores are borne within the sporangium. In *Ceratiomyxa*, spores are apparently borne externally; each, however, may be a much reduced sporangium with a true spore within.

Upon germination, a spore releases one or more individual cells known as myxamoebas, which may transform into so-called swarm cells with two flagella. The swarm cells often revert to the amoeboid stage. Formerly, it was believed that reproduction involved the nonsexual fusion of swarm cells, but the process is now thought to be sexual. The plasmodium, with cytoplasm streaming through it, changes shape as it crawls over or within damp wood, leaves, or soil, ingesting bacteria, molds, and fungi. Characteristically, the entire plasmodium is covered by a layer of slime, which is continually secreted and, as the plasmodium creeps, continually left behind as a network of collapsed tubules. Plasmodia are frequently yellow and orange, but they may also be colourless, red, white, buff, maroon, or, rarely, blue, black, or green.

OPALINID

Opalinids are protozoans found in the intestinal tracts of amphibians and some other animals. The nuclei of opalinids vary in number from two (e.g., *Zelleriella*) to many (e.g., *Cepedea*). The locomotor organelles (short, hairlike projections) are arranged in slanting, longitudinal rows. Species of the genus *Opalina* range from 90 to 500 micrometres (0.004 to 0.002 inches) in length. Reproduction is sexual by fusion of gametes (syngamy) or asexual by longitudinal splitting with distribution of the nuclei. Opalinids inhabit the intestines of amphibians (e.g., salamanders, newts) and some reptiles and fishes. They do not harm their host. Distribution is by encystment after reproduction. The cyst escapes in host feces and is ingested by another host. Opalinids are found worldwide, although species vary with location. One species, *Zelleriella opisthocarya*, is itself parasitized by another protozoan, *Entamoeba paulista*.

The taxonomic position of opalinids is uncertain, and they have been variously classified. Formerly considered a separate group, they were called Protociliata, but any close relationship to contemporary ciliate groups is now considered doubtful.

PARAMECIUM

Paramecium is a genus of free-living protozoans of the phylum Ciliophora. There are at least eight well-defined species, and all can be cultivated easily in the laboratory. Although they vary in size, most *Paramecium* species are about the size of the period at the end of this sentence. The basic shape varies, depending on the species: *P. caudatum* is elongated and gracefully streamlined and *P. bursaria* resembles a footprint. The term *paramecium* is also used to refer to individual organisms in a *Paramecium* species.

These microscopic single-celled organisms are completely covered with fine hairlike filaments (cilia) that beat rhythmically to propel them and to direct bacteria and other food particles into their mouths. On the ventral surface an oral groove runs diagonally posterior to the mouth and gullet. Within the gullet, food particles are transformed into food vacuoles, and digestion takes place within each food vacuole. Waste material is excreted through the anus.

A thin layer of clear, firm cytoplasm (ectoplasm) lies directly beneath the flexible body membrane (pellicle) and encloses the inner, more fluid portion of the cytoplasm (endoplasm), which contains gran-

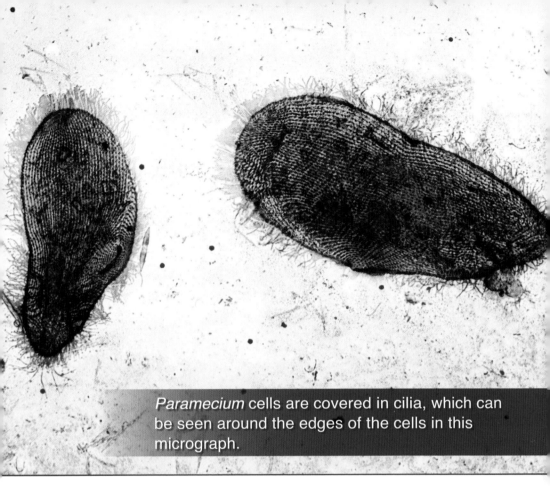

Paramecium cells are covered in cilia, which can be seen around the edges of the cells in this micrograph.

ules, food vacuoles, and crystals of different sizes. Embedded in the ectoplasm are spindle-shaped bodies (trichocysts) that may be released by chemical, electrical, or mechanical means. Originally believed to be a defense reaction, they appear to be extruded as a reaction to injury or for use as an anchoring device. A paramecium has two, occasionally three, contractile vacuoles located close to the surface near the ends of the cell. They function in regulating the water content within the cell and may also be considered excretory structures since the expelled water contains metabolic wastes.

Paramecia have two kinds of nuclei: a large ellipsoidal nucleus called a macronucleus and at least one small nucleus called a micronucleus. Both types of nuclei contain the full complement of genes that bear the hereditary information of the organism. The organism cannot survive without the macronucleus; it cannot reproduce without the micronucleus. The macronucleus is the centre of all metabolic activities of the organism. The micronucleus is a storage site for the genetic material of the organism. It gives rise to the macronucleus and is responsible for the genetic reorganization that occurs during conjugation (cross-fertilization).

Strictly speaking, the only type of reproduction in *Paramecium* is asexual binary fission in which a fully grown organism divides into two daughter cells. *Paramecium* also exhibits several types of sexual processes. Conjugation consists of the temporary union of two organisms and the exchange of micronuclear elements. Without the rejuvenating effects of conjugation, a paramecium ages and dies. Only opposite mating types, or genetically compatible organisms, can unite in conjugation. One species, *P. aurelia*, has 34 hereditary mating types that form 16 distinct mating groups, or syngens (now considered separate species by many authorities). Autogamy (self-fertilization) is a similar process that occurs in one animal. In cytogamy, another type of self-fertilization, two individuals join together but do not undergo nuclear exchange.

PLASMODIUM

Plasmodium is a genus of parasitic protozoans, which are known commonly as the causative organisms of malaria. *Plasmodium*, which infects red blood cells in mammals (including humans), birds, and reptiles, occurs worldwide, especially in tropical and temperate zones. The organism is transmitted by the bite of the female *Anopheles* mosquito. Other insects and some mites may also transmit forms of malaria to animals.

Five species cause human malaria: *P. vivax* (producing the most widespread form), *P. ovale* (relatively uncommon), *P. falciparum* (producing the most severe symptoms), *P. malariae*, and *P. knowlesi*. There are several species that have been isolated from chimpanzees, including *P. reichenowi* and *P. gaboni*. *P. falciparum*, *P. gaboni*, and other species have been isolated from gorillas. Examples of parasites found in reptiles include *P. mexicanum* and *P. floridense*, and those in birds include *P. relictum* and *P. juxtanucleare*.

Plasmodium species exhibit three life-cycle stages—gametocytes, sporozoites, and merozoites. Gametocytes within a mosquito develop into sporozoites. The sporozoites are transmitted via the saliva of a feeding mosquito to the human bloodstream. From there they enter liver parenchyma cells, where they divide and form merozoites. The

TREATING AND ERADICATING MALARIA

n the late 20th century, the incidence of malaria began to increase after having steadily declined for decades because some strains of *P. vivax* as well as most strains of *P. falciparum* had become resistant to drugs such as chloroquine, which were thus rendered ineffective.

Unlike some infectious diseases, infection with malaria induces the human body to develop immunity very slowly. Unprotected children in tropical countries acquire sufficient immunity to suppress clinical attacks only after many months or a few years of constant exposure to *Plasmodium* parasites by hungry mosquitoes. Even then, the immunity is effective only against the specific parasite to which the child has been exposed, and the immunity wanes after several months if the child is removed from constant exposure.

The first malaria vaccine to be approved was RTS,S (brand name Mosquirix), which was developed by GlaxoSmithKline and which gained approval in 2015 in Europe, enabling the World Health Organization (WHO) to formulate recommendations for its use in Africa. RTS,S was approved specifically for use in infants and young children aged 6 weeks to 17 months. In a study involving nearly 16,000 young children in Africa, the vaccine successfully prevented malarial infection in about 46 percent of young children aged 5 to 17 months and 27 percent of infants aged 6 to 12 weeks. RTS,S was a recombinant vaccine engineered to express *P. falciparum* proteins capable of stimulating antibody production against the parasite.

Other vaccines were also being studied. Of particular interest was a vaccine made of attenuated *P. falciparum* sporozoites (PfSPZ). In 2013 PfSPZ demonstrated early clinical success in protecting healthy volunteers against malaria. Individuals who received the highest doses of PfSPZ gained the highest levels of protection.

Another strategy was to develop an "antidisease" vaccine, which would block not the infection itself but rather the immune system's responses to infection, which are responsible for many of the harmful symptoms. A third approach, known as the "altruistic" vaccine, would not stop either infection or symptoms but would prevent infection from spreading to others by blocking the ability of the parasites to reproduce in the gut of the mosquito.

Despite progress on malaria vaccines, the mainstay of prevention in much of Africa and Southeast Asia is the insecticide-treated bed net, which has reduced mortality significantly in some areas. For example, in western Kenya the use of bed nets reduced mortality among children by 25 percent. Bed nets can be washed but must be re-treated with insecticide about every 6–12 months, depending on the frequency of washing. Long-lasting insecticide-treated nets (LLINs), in which insecticide forms a coating around the net's fibres or is incorporated into the fibres, can be used for at least three years before re-treatment is required.

(continued on the next page)

(continued from the previous page)

Frequent washing, however, may render LLINs less effective over time.

The most comprehensive method of prevention is to eliminate the breeding places of *Anopheles* mosquitoes by draining and filling marshes, swamps, stagnant pools, and other large or small bodies of standing freshwater. Insecticides have proved potent in controlling mosquito populations in affected areas.

In the early 21st century, declining numbers of malaria cases and deaths suggested that efforts to control the disease were working. According to WHO, the rate of new cases of malaria among populations at risk fell 21 percent between 2010 and 2015, and efforts to combat the disease have prevented an estimated 6.8 million deaths. However, there were still more than 400,000 deaths from malaria in 2015, most of them occurring in sub-Saharan Africa.

merozoites are released into the bloodstream and infect red blood cells. Rapid division of the merozoites results in the destruction of the red blood cells, and the newly multiplied merozoites then infect new red blood cells. Some merozoites may develop into gametocytes, which can be ingested by a feeding mosquito, starting the life cycle over again. The red blood cells destroyed by the merozoites liberate toxins that cause the periodic chill-and-fever cycles that are the typical symptoms of malaria. *P. vivax, P. ovale*, and *P. falciparum* repeat this chill-fever cycle every 48 hours (tertian malaria), and *P. malariae* repeats it every 72 hours (quartan malaria). *P. knowlesi* has a 24-hour life cycle and thus can cause daily spikes in fever.

RADIOLARIAN

Radiolarians are protozoans found in the upper layers of all oceans. They are mostly spherically symmetrical and are known for their complex and beautifully sculptured, though minute, skeletons, referred to as tests. Usually composed of silica, the test is elaborately perforated in a variety of patterns, forming a series either of lattice-like plates or of loose needle-shaped spicules. Pseudopodia extend through the perforated skeleton. A chitinous central capsule encloses the nuclei and divides the cytoplasm into two zones. The outer cytoplasm contains many vacuoles that control the organism's buoyancy.

Asexual reproduction is by budding, binary fission, or multiple fission. Generally, the skeleton divides, and each daughter cell regenerates the missing half. In some cases, however, one daughter cell escapes and develops an entirely new shell, the other daughter remaining within the parent skeleton.

The skeletal remains of radiolarians settle to the ocean floor and form radiolarian ooze. When the ocean bottom is lifted and transformed into land, the ooze becomes sedimentary rock. Silica deposits, such as flint, chert, and the abrasive tripoli, originate from radiolarian skeletons. Fossil radiolarians have been found that date to Precambrian time (3.96 billion to 540 million years ago).

SLIME MOLD

Slime molds are any of about 500 species of primitive organisms containing true nuclei and resembling both protozoan protists and fungi. The term *slime mold* embraces a heterogeneous assemblage of organisms whose juxtaposition reflects a historical confusion between superficial resemblances and actual relationships. The myxomycetes (true slime molds) are characterized by a plasmodial stage and definite fruiting bodies. Other slime molds include protostelids lids (minute, simple slime molds), acrasids (cellular slime molds), plasmodiophorids (parasitic slime molds), and labyrinthulids (net slime molds). Slime molds are found worldwide and typically thrive in dark, cool, moist conditions such as prevail on forest floors. Bacteria, yeast, molds, and fungi provide the main source of slime mold nutrition, although the plasmodiophorids feed parasitically on the roots of cabbage and other mustard family plants.

The life cycle of the myxomycetes is, allowing for minor variations, representative of that of slime molds generally. The cycle begins with a spore that has a diameter of 4 to 15 micrometres (0.0001 to

0.0006 inches) and that, in the presence of water, releases a small mass of cytoplasm called a swarm cell. It is propelled by flagella until it comes in contact with a surface and puts forth pseudopods that allow it to creep along. In its creeping phase it resembles an amoeba and is known as a myxamoeba. Both swarm cells and myxamoebae function as sex cells (gametes), and the fusion of two such cells constitutes the reproductive act of myxomycetes that begins the next stage of growth, the plasmodium.

Fuligo septica is a slime mold in the Myxomycetes class, meaning it shares characteristics, such as fruiting bodies, with fungi.

As the flagella are permanently retracted, the fertilized cell begins to grow by repeated division of its nuclei. The plasmodium moves gradually in successive waves, creating a characteristic fan shape. A layer of slime, in some species similar to saliva or mucus, covers the whole plasmodium.

The most remarkable metamorphosis of the slime molds occurs next: the growth from the shapeless plasmodium to an intricately organized spore case, or sporangium. Droplets form at the cell wall and coalesce to form a cushion and then a stalk that can grow to be 1.25 cm (0.5 inch) wide and 2.5 cm (1 inch) tall. As the column changes to purple and then black, the sporangium forms at its tip, filled with the dark spores. The sporangium wall dries and disintegrates, allowing air currents or a sudden movement to release the spores and begin the cycle again.

STENTOR

Stentor is a genus of trumpet-shaped, contractile, uniformly ciliated protozoans. They are found in freshwater, either free-swimming or attached to submerged vegetation. *Stentor* assumes an oval or pear shape while swimming. At its larger end, *Stentor* has multiple ciliary membranelles spiraling around the region that leads to the mouth opening. It uses these cilia to sweep food particles into its cytostome. The species *S. coeruleus* is large (sometimes up to 2 mm [0.08 inch] long) and is predominantly blue from a blue pigment, stentorin, found in its ectoplasm. *Stentor* is remarkable for its regenerative powers; a small fragment less than one-hundredth of the volume of an adult can grow back into a complete organism. This capability has made *Stentor* a favourite subject for studies of regeneration in protozoans.

TRICHOMONAD

Trichomonads are zooflagellate protozoans that possess three to six flagella, one of which commonly trails or borders an undulating membrane. Most trichomonads inhabit the digestive systems of animals. They may be uninucleate or multinucleate. Reproduction is by division.

The genus *Trichomonas* is a common parasite in the digestive system of many animals. *Trichomonas* cells are pear-shaped and may have four flagella anteriorly and a fifth bordering the undulating membrane. A mouth and a basal rod (costa) are found along the membrane. An axostyle, a stiff rod of cytoplasm used for support, often protrudes posteriorly. Three species occur in humans: *T. hominis* in the intestine, *T. vaginalis* in the vagina, and *T. buccalis* in the mouth. *Tritrichomonas foetus* is a pathogenic form in cattle.

TRYPANOSOMA

Trypanosoma is a genus of parasitic zooflagellate protozoans. Adult trypanosomes are mainly blood parasites of vertebrates, especially fishes, birds, and mammals. Most species require an intermediate host (often an insect or a leech) to complete their life cycle. Sleeping sickness (also called African trypanosomiasis), for example, caused by *T. gambiense* or *T. rhodesiense*, is transmitted by tsetse flies. In South and Central America, *T. cruzi*, the agent of Chagas' disease, and the harmless *T. rangeli* are transmitted by bloodsucking insects. Other species of trypanosomes induce economically important diseases of livestock: nagana, surra, mal de caderas, and dourine.

VORTICELLA

Vorticella is a genus of ciliate protozoans that are bell-shaped or cylindrical. *Vorticella* possess a conspicuous ring of cilia on the oral end and a contractile unbranched stalk on the aboral end. Cilia usually are not found between the oral and aboral ends. *Vorticella* eat bacteria and small protozoans and live in fresh or salt water attached to aquatic plants, surface scum, submerged objects, or aquatic animals. Although vorticellas are often found in clusters, each stalk is fastened independently. The stalk consists of an external sheath that contains a fluid and a spirally arranged contractile thread. When the vorticella is contracted the stalk thread is shortened, and the sheath is coiled like a corkscrew.

Vorticella species reproduce by longitudinal fission. One of the two daughter cells retains the original stalk, and the other grows a temporary wreath of cilia at the aboral end and migrates. Propelled by these cilia, the migrant eventually grows a stalk, attaches to a substrate, and loses its temporary cilia. In conjugation one small special migrant (microconjugant) finds an attached vorticella (macroconjugant) and the two conjugants amalgamate completely, forming one organism in a sex-like union that eventually leads to fission.

ZOOFLAGELLATE

Zooflagellates are flagellated protozoans that assimilate organic material by osmotrophy (absorption through the plasma membrane) or phagotrophy (engulfing prey in food vacuoles). These organisms traditionally were considered members of the protozoan class Zoomastigophorea (sometimes called Zooflagellata). However, recent classifications of this group have questioned the taxonomic usefulness of the term because some zooflagellates have been found to have photosynthetic capabilities and some phytoflagellates heterotrophic capabilities.

The zooflagellate's flexible pellicle (envelope) is sufficiently thin in certain genera to permit pseudo-podal projections. Zooflagellates exhibit a consider-able variation in form, and they may be free-living, symbiotic, commensal, or parasitic in humans and other animals and in certain plants.

CHAPTER

6

FEATURES OF ALGAE

Algae are eukaryotic and predominantly aquatic photosynthetic organisms. They range in size from the tiny flagellate *Micromonas* that is 1 micrometre (0.000039 inch) in diameter to giant kelps that reach 60 metres (200 feet) in length. Algae provide much of Earth's oxygen, they are the food base for almost all aquatic life, they are a source of crude oil, and they provide foods and pharmaceutical and industrial products for humans. The algae have many types of life cycles. Their photosynthetic pigments are more varied than those of plants, and their cells have features not found among plants and animals. Some groups of algae are ancient, whereas other groups appear to have evolved more recently. The taxonomy of algae is subject to rapid change because new information is constantly being discovered.

The study of algae is termed *phycology*, and one who studies algae is known as a *phycologist*.

Although algae are photosynthetic organisms, they lack the specialized reproductive structures of plants, which always have multicellular reproductive structures that contain fertile gamete-producing cells surrounded by sterile cells. Algae also lack true roots, stems, and leaves—features they share with plants known as bryophytes (e.g., mosses and liverworts).

Algae can spread rapidly across the surface of lakes and ponds, creating what is known as an algal bloom.

In the past, the prokaryotic (nucleus-lacking) cyanobacteria (blue-green algae), a group that includes photosynthetic marine organisms in the genus *Prochlorococcus*, were considered to be algae. Beginning in the 1970s, some scientists suggested that the study of the prokaryotic algae should be incorporated into the study of bacteria because of certain shared cellular features. In fact, today cyanobacteria and *Prochlorococcus* are known to be more closely related to bacteria than to algae, and for this reason they are now classified with the bacteria. However, because of their oxygen-producing photosynthetic capability, they sometimes are included in discussions about algae.

Beginning in the 1830s, algae were classified into major groups based on colour (e.g., red, brown, and green). The colours are a reflection of different chloroplast pigments, such as chlorophylls, carotenoids, and phycobiliproteins. Many more than three groups of pigments are recognized, and each class of algae shares a common set of pigment types distinct from those of all other groups.

The algae are not closely related in an evolutionary sense. Specific groups of algae share features with protozoa and fungi that, without the presence of chloroplasts and photosynthesis as delimiting features, make them difficult to distinguish from certain members of these groups. Thus, some algae appear to have a closer evolutionary relationship with the protozoa or fungi than they do with other algae, and, conversely, some protozoa or fungi are more closely related to algae than to other protozoa or fungi.

Knowledge and use of algae are perhaps as old as humankind. Seaweeds are still eaten by some coastal peoples, and algae are considered acceptable foods in many restaurants. Many slimy rocks are covered with algae such as diatoms or cyanophytes, and algae are the cause of green or golden sheens on pools and ponds. Algae are the base of the food chain for all marine organisms since few other kinds of plants live in the oceans.

Algae possess a number of distinct physical and ecological features. For example, their tremendous size range and their abundance within aquatic habitats are remarkable. In most instances, algae are uniquely adapted physically to their habitats, and this has resulted in a vast array of algal forms, all of which have important ecological functions. The majority of algae fulfill beneficial roles, not only within nature but also within human societies. Thus, from serving as the base of aquatic food chains to being used for the production of foods and medicines for humans, algae are important both ecologically and commercially.

SIZE RANGE AND DISTRIBUTION

The size range of the algae spans seven orders of magnitude. Many algae consist of only one cell, others have two or more cells, and the largest have millions of cells. In large, macroscopic algae, groups of cells are specialized for specific functions, such as anchorage, transport, photosynthesis, and reproduction. Specialization involving thousands of cells indicates a measure of complexity and evolutionary advancement.

The algae can be divided into several types based on the morphology of their vegetative, or growing, state. Filamentous forms have cells arranged in chains like strings of beads. Some filaments (e.g., *Spirogyra*) are unbranched, whereas others (e.g., *Stigeoclonium*) are branched and bushlike. In many red algae (e.g., *Palmaria*), numerous adjacent filaments joined laterally create the gross morphological form of the alga. Parenchymatous (tissue-like) forms, such as the giant kelp *Macrocystis*, can be very large, measuring many metres in length. Coenocytic forms of algae grow to large sizes without forming distinct cells. Coenocytic algae are essentially unicellular, multinucleated algae in which the protoplasm (cytoplasmic and nuclear content of a cell) is not subdivided by cell walls. The green seaweed *Codium*, which has been called dead-man's-fingers, is an example of this.

Some algae have flagella and swim through the water. These flagellates range from single cells, such as *Ochromonas*, to colonial organisms with thousands of cells, such as *Volvox*. Coccoid organisms, such as

Scenedesmus, normally have an exact number of cells per colony, produced by a series of rapid cell divisions when the organism is first formed. Once the exact cell number is obtained, the organism grows in size but not in cell number. Capsoid organisms, such as *Chryso-capsa*, have variable numbers of cells. These cells are found in clusters that increase gradually in cell number and are embedded in transparent gel.

Algae are almost ubiquitous throughout the world, being most common in aquatic habitats. They

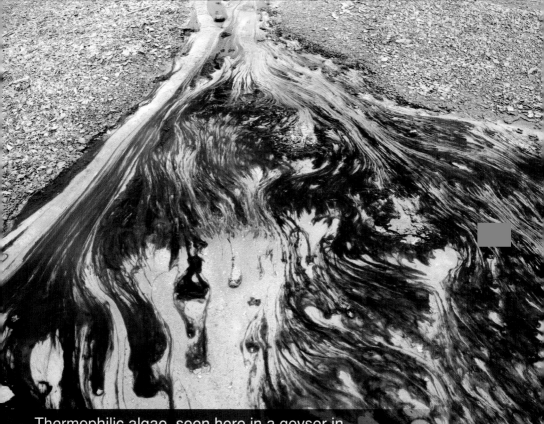

Thermophilic algae, seen here in a geyser in Yellowstone National Park, can survive in the high temperatures of hot springs.

can be categorized ecologically by their habitats. Planktonic microscopic algae grow suspended in the water, whereas neustonic algae grow on the water surface. Cryophilic algae occur in snow and ice; thermophilic algae live in hot springs; edaphic algae live on or in soil; epizoic algae grow on animals, such as turtles and sloths; epiphytic algae grow on fungi, land plants, or other algae; corticolous algae grow on the bark of trees; epilithic algae live on rocks; endolithic algae live in porous rocks; and chasmolithic algae grow in rock fissures. Some algae live inside other organisms, and in a general sense these are called endosymbionts. Specifically, endozoic endosymbionts live in protozoa or other, larger animals, whereas endophytic endosymbionts live in fungi, lichens, plants, or other algae.

Algal abundance and diversity vary from one environment to the next, just as land plant abundance and diversity vary from tropical forests to deserts. Terrestrial vegetation (plants and algae) is influenced most by precipitation and temperature, whereas aquatic vegetation (primarily algae) is influenced most by light and nutrients. When nutrients are abundant, as in some polluted waters, algal cell numbers can become great enough to produce obvious patches of algae called "blooms" or "red tides," usually linked to favourable growing conditions, including an abundance of nutrients.

ECOLOGICAL IMPORTANCE OF ALGAE

Algae form organic food molecules from carbon dioxide and water through the process of photosynthesis, in which they capture energy from sunlight. Similar to land plants, algae are at the base of the food chain, and the existence of nonphotosynthetic organisms is dependent upon the presence of photosynthetic organisms. Nearly three-fourths of Earth is covered by water, and since the so-called higher plants are virtually absent from the major water sources (e.g., the oceans), the existence of nearly all marine life—including whales, seals, fishes, turtles, shrimps, lobsters, clams, octopuses, starfish, and worms—ultimately depends upon algae. In addition to making organic molecules, algae produce oxygen as a by-product of photosynthesis. Algae produce an estimated 30 to 50 percent of the net global oxygen available to humans and other terrestrial animals for respiration.

Crude oil and natural gas are the remnants of photosynthetic products of ancient algae, which were subsequently modified by bacteria. The North Sea oil deposits are believed to have been formed from coccolithophore algae, and the Colorado oil shales by an alga similar to *Botryococcus* (a green alga). Today, *Botryococcus* produces blooms in Lake Baikal where it releases so much oil onto the surface of the lake that it can be collected with a special skimming apparatus and used as a source of fuel. Several companies have grown oil-producing algae in high-salinity ponds and have extracted the oil as a potential alternative to fossil fuels.

COMMERCIAL IMPORTANCE

Algae, as processed and unprocessed food, have an annual commercial value of several billion dollars. Algal extracts are commonly used in preparing foods and other products, and the direct consumption of algae has existed for centuries in the diets of East Asian and Pacific Island societies. Many species of algae, including *Porphyra umbilicaria* (nori, or laver) and *Palmaria palmata* (dulse), are eaten by humans. The red alga *Porphyra* is the most important commercial food alga. In Japan alone approximately 100,000 hectares (247,000 acres) of shallow bays and seas are farmed. *Porphyra* has two major stages in its life cycle: the *Conchocelis* stage and the *Porphyra* stage. The *Conchocelis* is a small, shell-boring stage that can be artificially propagated by seeding on oyster shells that are tied to ropes or nets and set out in special marine beds for further development. The conchospores that germinate grow into the large blades of *Porphyra* plants, which in due course are removed from the nets, washed, sometimes chopped, and pressed into sheets to dry.

Palmaria palmata, another red alga, is eaten primarily in the North Atlantic region. Known as dulse in Canada and the United States, as *duileasg* (dulisk) in Scotland, as *duileasc* (dillisk) in Ireland, and as *söl* in Iceland, it is harvested by hand from intertidal rocks during low tide. Species of *Laminaria*, *Undaria*, and

Hizikia (a type of brown algae) are also harvested from wild beds along rocky shores, particularly in Japan, Korea, and China, where they may be eaten with meat or fish and in soups. The green algae *Monostroma* and *Ulva* look somewhat like leaves of lettuce (their common name is sea lettuce) and are eaten as salads or in soups, relishes, and meat or fish dishes.

The microscopic, freshwater green alga *Chlorella* is cultivated as a food supplement and is eaten in Taiwan, Japan, Malaysia, and the Philippines. It has a high protein content (53 to 65 percent) and has even been considered as a possible food source during extended space travel.

The cell walls of many seaweeds contain phycocolloids (algal colloids) that can be extracted by hot water. The three major phycocolloids are alginates, agars, and carrageenans. Alginates are extracted primarily from brown seaweeds, and agar and carrageenan are extracted from red seaweeds. These phycocolloids are polymers of chemically modified sugar molecules, such as galactose in agars and carrageenans, or organic acids, such as mannuronic acid and glucuronic acid in alginates. Most phycocolloids can be safely consumed by humans and other animals, and many are used in a wide variety of prepared foods, such as "ready-mix" cakes, "instant" puddings and pie fillings, and artificial dairy toppings. Alginates, or alginic acids, commercially extracted from brown seaweeds, such as *Macrocystis*, *Laminaria*, and *Ascophyllum*, are used in ice creams to limit ice crystal formation (producing a smooth texture), in syrups as emulsifiers and thickeners, and in candy bars and salad dressings as fillers. In addition to their important role as food products, phycocolloids have industrial uses. They are relatively inert and are used as creams and gels in medical drugs and insecticides.

Agars, extracted primarily from species of red algae, such as *Gelidium*, *Gracilaria*, *Pterocladia*, *Acanthopeltis*, and *Ahnfeltia*, are used in instant pie fillings, canned meats or fish, and bakery icings and for clarifying beer and wine. Agar is used extensively in laboratory research as a substrate for growing bacteria, fungi, and algae in pure cultures and as a substrate for eukaryotic cell culture and tissue culture.

Carrageenans are extracted from various red algae, including *Eucheuma* in the Philippines, *Chondrus* (also called Irish moss) in the United States and the Canadian Maritime Provinces, and *Iridaea* in Chile. Carrageenans are used for thickening and stabilizing dairy products, imitation creams, puddings, syrups, and canned pet foods. They are also used in the manufacture of shampoos, cosmetics, and medicines.

The diatoms played an important role in industrial development during the 20th century. The frustules, or cell walls, of diatoms are made of opaline silica and contain many fine pores. Large quantities of frustules are deposited in some ocean and lake sediments, and their fossilized remains are called diatomite. Diatomite contains approximately 3,000 diatom frustules per cubic millimetre (50 million diatom frustules per cubic inch). When geologic uplifting brings deposits of diatomite above sea level, the diatomite is easily mined. A deposit located in Lompoc, Calif., U.S., for example, covers 13 square kilometres (5 square miles) and is up to 425 metres (1,400 feet) deep.

Diatomite is relatively inert and has a high absorptive capacity, large surface area, and low bulk density. It consists of approximately 90 percent silica, and the remainder consists of compounds such as aluminum and iron oxides. The fine pores in the diatom frustules make diatomite an excellent filtering material for beverages (e.g., fruit juices, soft drinks, beer, and wine), chemicals (e.g., sodium hydroxide, sulfuric acid, and gold salts), industrial oils (e.g., those used as lubricants in rolling mills or for cutting), cooking oils (e.g., vegetable and animal), sugars (e.g., cane, beet, and corn), water supplies (e.g., municipal, swimming pool, waste, and boiler), varnishes, lacquers, jet fuels, and antibiotics, as well as many other products. Its relatively low abrasive properties make it suitable for use in toothpaste, sink cleansers, polishes (for silver and automobiles), and buffing compounds.

Diatomite is also widely used as a filler and extender in paint, paper, rubber, and plastic products. The gloss and sheen of "flat" paints can be controlled by the use of various additions of diatomite. During the manufacture of plastic bags, diatomite can be added to the newly formed sheets to act as an antiblocking agent so that the plastic (polyethylene) can be rolled while it is still hot. Because it can absorb approximately 2.5 times its weight in water, it also makes an excellent anticaking carrier for powders used to dust roses or for cleansers used to clean rugs. Diatomite is also used in making welding rods, battery boxes, concrete, explosives, and animal foods.

Chalk is another fossilized deposit of remains of protists. It consists in part of calcium carbonate scales, or coccoliths, from the coccolithophore members of Haptophyta. Chalk deposits, such as the white cliffs in Dover, Kent, Eng., contain large amounts of coccoliths, as well as the shells of foraminiferan protozoa. Coccoliths can be observed in fragments of ordinary blackboard chalk examined under a light microscope.

By the end of the 18th century, kelps were harvested and burned to produce soda. When mineral deposits containing soda were discovered in Salzburg, Austria, and elsewhere, the use of kelp ash declined. Kelps were again harvested in abundance during the 19th century when salts and iodine were

Seaweed farmers harvest seaweed by placing posts in the water and stringing ropes between them. The seaweed then collects on the ropes, making it easy for the farmers to gather.

extracted for commercial use, although the discovery of cooking salt and iodides led to a demise of the kelp industry. During World War I the United States used seaweeds to produce potash, a plant fertilizer, and acetone, a necessary component in the manufacture of smokeless gunpowder.

For many centuries, seaweeds around the world have been widely used as agricultural fertilizers. Coastal farmers collect seaweeds by cutting them from seaweed beds growing in the ocean or by gathering them from masses washed up on shores after storms. The seaweeds are then spread over the soil. Dried seaweed, although almost 50 percent mineral matter, contains a large amount of nitrogenous organic matter. Commercial extracts of seaweed sold as plant fertilizers contain a mixture of macronutrients, micronutrients, and trace elements that promote robust plant growth.

The green unicellular flagellate *Dunaliella*, which turns red when physiologically stressed, is cultivated in saline ponds for the production of carotene and glycerol. These compounds can be produced in large amounts and extracted and sold commercially.

TOXICITY

Some algae can be harmful to humans. A few species produce toxins that may be concentrated in shellfish and finfish, which are thereby rendered unsafe or poisonous for human consumption. The dinoflagellates are the most notorious producers of toxins. Paralytic shellfish poisoning is caused by saxitoxin or any of at least 12 related compounds. Saxitoxin is probably the most toxic compound known; it is 100,000 times more toxic than cocaine. Saxitoxin and saxitoxin-like compounds are nerve toxins that interfere with neuromuscular function. *Alexandrium tamarense* and *Gymnodinium catenatum* are the two species most often associated with paralytic shellfish poisoning. Diarrheic shellfish poisoning is caused by okadaic acids that are produced by several kinds of algae,

Algal blooms can be toxic to marine animals and birds. Here a volunteer helps give fluids to poisoned sea lions in California.

especially species of *Dinophysis*. Neurotoxic shellfish poisoning, caused by toxins produced in *Gymnodinium breve*, an organism associated with red tides, is notorious for fish kills and shellfish poisoning along the coast of Florida in the United States. When the red tide blooms are blown to shore, wind-sprayed toxic cells can cause health problems for humans and other animals that breathe the air.

Ciguatera is a disease of humans caused by consumption of tropical fish that have fed on the alga *Gambierdiscus* or *Ostreopsis*. Unlike many other dinoflagellate toxins, ciguatoxin and maitotoxin are concentrated in finfish rather than shellfish. Levels as low as one part per billion in fish can be sufficient to cause human intoxication.

Not all shellfish poisons are produced by dino-flagellates. Amnesic shellfish poisoning is caused by domoic acid, which is produced by diatoms, such as *Nitzschia pungens* and *Nitzschia pseudodelicatissima*. Symptoms of this poisoning in humans progress from abdominal cramps to vomiting to memory loss to disorientation and finally to death.

Several algae produce toxins lethal to fish. *Prymnesium parvum* has caused massive die-offs in ponds where fish are cultured, and *Chrysochromulina polylepis* has caused major fish kills along the coasts of the Scandinavian countries. Other algae, such as *Heterosigma* and *Dictyocha*, are suspected fish killers as well.

Algae can cause human diseases by directly attacking human tissues, although the frequency is rare. Prototothecosis, caused by the chloroplast-lacking green alga, *Prototheca*, can result in waterlogged skin lesions, in which the pathogen grows. *Prototheca* organisms may eventually spread to the lymph glands from these subcutaneous lesions. *Prototheca* is also believed to be responsible for ulcerative dermatitis in the platypus. Very rarely, similar infections in humans and cattle can be caused by chloroplast-bearing species of *Chlorella*.

Some seaweeds contain high concentrations of arsenic and when eaten may cause arsenic poisoning. For example, the brown alga *Hizikia* contains sufficient arsenic to be used as a rat poison.

Diatoms have been used in forensic medicine. In cases in which death by drowning is suspected, lung tissue and blood vessels are examined. The presence of siliceous diatom walls, transported in the bloodstream of the dying persons, is evidence for death by drowning. Certain diatom species can even be used to pinpoint the location of death insofar as they are characteristic for a given body of water.

FORM AND FUNCTION

Similar to other protists, the cells of algae contain membrane-bound organelles, and some algae have flagella, which provide an important means of locomotion. The mechanisms of cell division and of energy production vary among the different groups of algae. In addition, their photosynthetic pigments are more diverse than those of plants, and their cells have features not found among plants and animals.

ALGAL CELL FEATURES

Most eukaryotic algal cells contain three types of double membrane-bound organelles: the nucleus, the chloroplast, and the mitochondrion. In most algal cells there is only a single nucleus, although some cells are multinucleate. In addition, some algae are siphonaceous, with many nuclei not separated by cell walls. The nucleus contains most of the genetic material, or DNA (deoxyribonucleic acid), of the cell. In most algae, the molecules of DNA exist as linear strands that are condensed into obvious chromosomes only at the time of nuclear division (mitosis). However, there are certain groups of algae (e.g., dinophytes) in which the nuclear DNA is always condensed into chromosomes. In all algae, the two membranes that surround the nucleus are referred to as the nuclear envelope. The nuclear envelope typically has specialized nuclear pores that regulate the movement of molecules into and out of the nucleus.

Chloroplasts are the sites of photosynthesis, the complex set of biochemical reactions that use the energy of light to convert carbon dioxide and water into sugars. Each chloroplast contains flattened, membranous sacs, called thylakoids, that contain the photosynthetic light-harvesting pigments, the chlorophylls, carotenoids, and phycobiliproteins.

The mitochondria are the sites where food molecules are broken down and carbon dioxide, water, and chemical bond energy are released, a process called cellular respiration. Photosynthesis and respiration are approximately opposite processes, the former building sugar molecules and the latter breaking them down. The inner membrane of the mitochondrion is infolded to a great extent, and this provides the surface area necessary for respiration. The infoldings, called cristae, have three morphologies: (1) flattened or sheetlike, (2) fingerlike or tubular, and (3) paddle-like.

The mitochondria of land plants and animals, by comparison, generally have flattened cristae.

Chloroplasts and mitochondria also have their own DNA. However, this DNA is not like nuclear DNA in that it is circular (or, more correctly, in endless loops) rather than linear and therefore resembles the DNA of prokaryotes. The similarity of chloroplastic and mitochondrial DNA to prokaryotic DNA has led many scientists to accept the hypothesis of endosymbiosis, which states that these organelles developed as a result of a long and successful symbiotic association of prokaryote cells inside eukaryote host cells.

Algal cells also have several single-membrane-bound organelles, including the endoplasmic reticulum, Golgi apparatus, lysosomes, peroxisomes, contractile or noncontractile vacuoles, and, in some, ejectile organelles. The endoplasmic reticulum is a complex membranous system that forms intracellular compartments, acts as a transport system within the cell, and serves as a site for synthesizing fats, oils, and proteins. The Golgi apparatus, a series of flattened, membranous sacs that are arranged in a stack, performs four distinct functions: it sorts many molecules synthesized elsewhere in the cell; it produces carbohydrates, such as cellulose or sugars, and sometimes attaches the sugars to other molecules; it packages molecules in small vesicles; and it marks the vesicles so that they are routed to the proper destination. The lysosome is a specialized vacuole that contains digestive enzymes that break down old organelles, cells or cellular components during certain developmental stages, and particulate matter that is ingested in species that can engulf food. Peroxisomes specialize in metabolically breaking down certain organic molecules and dangerous compounds, such as hydrogen peroxide, that may be produced during some biochemical reactions.

Vacuoles are membranous sacs that store many different substances, depending on the organism and its metabolic state. Contractile vacuoles are specialized organelles that regulate the water content of cells and are therefore not involved in the long-term storage of substances. When too much water enters the cells, contractile vacuoles serve to "squirt" it out. Some algae have special ejectile organelles that apparently act as protective structures. Dinophytes have harpoon-like trichocysts beneath the cell surface that can explode from a disturbed or irritated cell. Trichocysts may serve to attach prey to algae cells before the prey is consumed. Ejectosomes are structures that are analogous to ejectile organelles and are found in algae known as cryptophytes. Several types of algae have mucous organelles that secrete slime. *Gonyostomum semen*, a freshwater alga, has numerous mucocysts, which, when such cells are collected in a plankton net, discharge and render the net and its contents somewhat gummy.

The nonmembrane-bound organelles of algae include the ribosomes, pyrenoids, microtubules, and microfilaments. Ribosomes are the sites of protein synthesis, where genetic information in the form of messenger ribonucleic acid (mRNA) is translated into protein. The ribosomes accurately interpret the genetic code of the DNA so that each protein is made exactly to the genetic specifications. The pyrenoid, a dense structure inside or beside chloroplasts of certain algae, consists largely of ribulose biphosphate carboxylase, one of the enzymes necessary in photosynthesis for carbon fixation and thus sugar formation. Starch, a storage form of glucose, is often found around pyrenoids. Microtubules, tubelike structures formed from tubulin proteins, are present in most cells. In many algae, microtubules appear and disappear as needed. Microtubules provide a rigid structure, or cytoskeleton, in the cell that helps determine and maintain the shape of the cell, especially in species without cell walls. Microtubules also provide a sort of "rail" system along which vesicles are transported. The spindle apparatus, which separates the chromosomes during nuclear division, consists of microtubules. Finally, certain kinds of microtubules also form the basic structure, or axoneme, of a flagellum, and they are a major component of the root system that anchors a flagellum within the cell. Microfilaments are formed by the polymerization of proteins such as actin, which can contract and relax and therefore function as tiny muscles inside the cells.

FLAGELLA

A flagellum is structurally complex, containing more than 250 types of proteins. Each flagellum consists of an axoneme, or cylinder, with nine outer pairs of microtubules surrounding two central microtubules. The axoneme is surrounded by a membrane, sometimes beset by hairs or scales. The outer pairs of microtubules are connected to the axoneme by a protein called nexin. Each of the nine outer pairs of microtubules has an *a* tubule and a *b* tubule. The *a* tubule has numerous molecules of a protein called dynein that are attached along its length. Extensions of dynein, called dynein arms, connect neighbouring tubules, forming dynein cross-bridges. Dynein is involved in converting the chemical energy of adenosine triphosphate (ATP) into the mechanical energy that mediates flagellar movement. In the presence of ATP, dynein molecules are activated, and the flagellum bends as dynein arms on one side of a dynein crossbridge become activated and move up the microtubule. This creates the power stroke. The dynein arms on the opposite side of the dynein cross-bridge are then activated and slide up the opposite microtubule. This causes the flagellum to bend in the opposite direction during the recovery stroke. Although scientists are working to discover the additional mechanisms that are involved in producing the whiplike movement characteristic of many eukaryotic flagella, the importance of dynein activation in this process has been established.

The flagellum membrane is also complex. It may contain special receptors called chemoreceptors that respond to chemical stimuli and allow the algal cell to recognize a multitude of signals, ranging from signals carrying information about changes in the alga's environment to signals carrying information about mating partners. On some flagella, superficial scales and hairs may aid in swimming. Certain swellings and para-axonemal structures, such as crystalline rods and noncrystalline rods and sheets, may be involved in photoreception, providing the swimming cell with a means for detecting light. The flagellum membrane merges into the cell membrane, where the nine pairs of axonemal microtubules enter the main body of the cell. At this junction, each pair of microtubules is joined by an additional microtubule, forming nine triplets. This cylinder of nine triplets, constituting the basal body, anchors the flagellum in the cell membrane. The anchorage provided by the basal body is strengthened by muscle-like fibres and special microtubules called microtubular roots. Most flagellate cells have two flagella, and therefore two basal bodies, each

with microtubular roots. The orientation of the flagella and the arrangement of the muscle-like fibres
and microtubular roots are important taxonomic
features that can be used to classify algae.

MITOSIS

Mitosis, or the process of replication and division of
the nucleus that results in the production of genetically identical daughter cells, is relatively similar
among plants and animals, but the algae have a
wide diversity of mitotic features that not only set the
algae apart from plants and animals but also set certain algae apart from other algae. The nuclear envelope breaks apart in some algal groups but remains
intact in others. The spindle microtubules remain
outside the nucleus in some algae, enter the nucleus
through holes in the nuclear envelope in other algae,
and form inside the nucleus and nuclear envelope in
still other algae. The diversity and complexity of algal
mitosis provide clues to a better understanding of
how mitosis operates in higher plants and animals.

CELLULAR RESPIRATION

Cellular respiration in algae, as in all organisms, is the
process by which food molecules are metabolized
to obtain chemical energy for the cell. Most algae
are aerobic (i.e., they live in the presence of oxygen),

although a few euglenophytes can live anaerobically in environments without oxygen. The biochemical pathways for respiration in algae are similar to those of other eukaryotes. The initial breakdown of food molecules, such as sugars, fatty acids, and proteins, occurs in the cytoplasm, but the final high energy-releasing steps occur inside the mitochondria.

LIGHT ABSORBTION

Photosynthesis is the process by which light energy is converted to chemical energy, whereby carbon dioxide and water are converted into organic molecules. The process occurs in almost all algae, and in fact much of what is known about photosynthesis was first discovered by studying the green alga *Chlorella*.

Photosynthesis comprises both light reactions and dark reactions (the Calvin cycle). During the dark reactions, carbon dioxide is bound to ribulose bisphosphate, a 5-carbon sugar with two attached phosphate groups, by the enzyme ribulose bisphosphate carboxylase. This is the initial step of a complex process leading to the formation of sugars. During the light reactions, light energy is converted into the chemical energy needed for the dark reactions.

The light reactions of many algae differ from those of land plants because some of them use different pigments to harvest light. Chlorophylls absorb primarily blue and red light, whereas carotenoids absorb primarily blue and green light, and phycobiliproteins absorb primarily blue or red light.

Since the amount of light absorbed depends upon the pigment composition and concentration found in the alga, some algae absorb more light at a given wavelength, and therefore, potentially, those algae can convert more light energy of that wavelength to chemical energy via photosynthesis. All algae use chlorophyll *a* to collect photosynthetically active light. Green algae and euglenophytes also use chlorophyll *b*. In addition to chlorophyll *a*, the remaining algae also use various combinations of other chlorophylls, chlorophyllides, carotenoids, and phycobiliproteins to collect additional light from wavelengths of the spectrum not absorbed by chlorophyll *a* or *b*. The chromophyte algae, dinoflagellates, cryptomonads, and the genus *Micromonas*, for example, also use chlorophyllides. (Chlorophyllides, often incorrectly called chlorophylls, differ from true chlorophylls in that they lack the long, fat-soluble phytol tail that is characteristic of chlorophylls.) Some green algae use carotenoids for harvesting photosynthetically active light, but the dinophyte and chromophyte algae almost always use carotenoids. Phycobiliproteins, which appear either blue (phycocyanins) or red (phycoerythrins), are found in red algae and cryptomonads.

Red wavelengths are absorbed in the first few metres of water. Blue wavelengths are more readily absorbed if the water contains average or abundant amounts of organic material. Thus, green wavelengths are often the most common light in deep water. Chlorophylls absorb red and blue wavelengths much more strongly than they absorb green wavelengths, which is why chlorophyll-bearing plants appear green. The carotenoids and phycobiliproteins, on the other hand, strongly absorb green wavelengths. Algae with large amounts of carotenoid appear yellow to brown, those with large amounts of phycocyanin appear blue, and those with large amounts of phycoerythrin appear red.

At one time it was believed that algae with specialized green-absorbing accessory pigments outcompeted green algae in deeper water. Some green algae, however, grow as well as other algae in deep water, and the deepest attached algae include green algae. The explanation of this paradox is that the cell structure of the deepwater green algae is designed to capture virtually all light, green or otherwise. Thus, while green-absorbing pigments are advantageous in deeper waters, evolutionary changes in cell structure can evidently compensate for the absence of these pigments.

NUTRIENT STORAGE

As in land plants, the major carbohydrate storage product of the green algae is usually starch in the form of amylose or amylopectin. These starches are polysaccharides in which the monomer, or fundamental unit, is glucose. Green algal starch comprises more than 1,000 sugar molecules, joined by alpha linkages between the number 1 and number 4 carbon atoms. The cell walls of many, but not all, algae contain cellulose. Cellulose is formed from similar glucose molecules but with beta linkages between the number 1 and 4 carbons. The cryptophytes also store amylose and amylopectin. These starches are stored outside the chloroplast but within the surrounding membranes of the chloroplast endoplasmic reticulum. Most dinophytes store starch outside the chloroplast, often as a cap over a bulging pyrenoid. The major carbohydrate storage product of red algae is a type of starch molecule (Floridean starch) that is more highly branched than amylopectin. Floridean starch is stored as grains outside the chloroplast.

The major carbohydrate storage product of the chromophyte algae is formed from glucose molecules interconnected with beta linkages between the number 1 and 3 carbons. These polysaccharide compounds are always stored outside the chloroplast. The number of glucose units in each storage product varies among the algal classes, and each type is given a special name—i.e., chrysolaminarin in diatoms, laminarin in brown algae, leucosin in chrysophytes, and paramylon in euglenophytes. The exact chemical constituency of the major polysaccharide storage products remains unknown for a number of algae. In the chromophyte algae, the molecules are usually small (16–40 units of sugar) and are stored in solution in vacuoles, whereas in the euglenophyte algae, the molecules of paramylon are large (approximately 150 units of sugar) and are stored as grains.

Not all algae have chloroplasts and photosynthesize. "Colourless" algae can obtain energy and food by oxidizing organic molecules, which they absorb from the environment or digest from engulfed particles. They are classified as algae, rather than fungi or protozoa, because in most other features they resemble photosynthetic algae. Algae that rely on ingestion and oxidation of organic molecules are referred to as heterotrophic algae because they depend on the organic materials produced by other organisms. Algae also produce many other kinds of sugars and sugar alcohols, such as rhamnose, trehalose, and xylose, and some algae can generate energy by oxidizing these molecules.

REPRODUCTION AND LIFE CYCLES

Algae regenerate by sexual reproduction, involving male and female gametes (sex cells), by asexual reproduction, or by both ways. Asexual reproduction is the production of progeny without the union of cells or nuclear material. Many small algae reproduce asexually by ordinary cell division or by fragmentation, whereas larger algae reproduce by spores. Some red algae produce monospores (walled, nonflagellate, spherical cells) that are carried by water currents and upon germination produce a new organism. Some green algae produce nonmotile spores called aplanospores. In contrast, zoospores lack true cell walls and bear one or more flagella. These flagella allow zoospores to swim to a favourable environment, whereas monospores and aplanospores have to rely on passive transport by water currents.

Sexual reproduction is characterized by the process of meiosis, in which progeny cells receive half of their genetic information from each parent cell. Sexual reproduction is usually regulated by environmental events. In many species, when temperature, salinity, inorganic nutrients (e.g., phosphorus, nitrogen, and magnesium), or day length become unfavourable, sexual reproduction is induced. A sexually reproducing alga typically has two phases in its life cycle. In the first stage, each cell has a single set of chromosomes and is called haploid, whereas in the second stage each cell has two sets of chromosomes and is called diploid. When one haploid gamete fuses with another haploid gamete during fertilization, the resulting combination, with two sets of chromosomes, is called a zygote. Either immediately or at some later time, a diploid cell directly or indirectly undergoes a special reductive cell-division process (meiosis). Diploid cells in this stage are called sporophytes because they produce spores. During meiosis the chromosome number of a diploid sporophyte is halved, and the resulting daughter cells are haploid. At some time, immediately or later, haploid cells act directly as gametes. In algae, as in plants, haploid cells in this stage are called gametophytes because they produce gametes.

The life cycles of sexually reproducing algae vary. In some, the dominant stage is the sporophyte, whereas in others it is the gametophyte. For example, *Sargassum* has a diploid (sporophyte) body, and the haploid phase is represented by gametes. *Ectocarpus* has alternating diploid and haploid vegetative stages, whereas *Spirogyra* has a haploid vegetative stage, and the zygote is the only diploid cell. In freshwater organisms especially, the fertilized egg, or zygote, often passes into a dormant state called a zygospore. Zygospores generally have a large store of food reserves and a thick, resistant cell wall. Following an appropriate environmental stimulus, such as a change in light, temperature, or nutrients, the zygospores are induced to germinate and start another period of growth. Most algae can live for days, weeks, or months. Small algae are sometimes found in abundance during a short period of the year and remain dormant during the rest of the year. In some species, the dormant form is a resistant cyst, whereas other species remain in the vegetative state but at very low population numbers. Some large, attached species are true perennials. They may lose the main body at the end of the growing season, but the attachment part, the holdfast, produces new growth only at the beginning of the next growing season.

The red algae, as exemplified by *Polysiphonia*, have some of the most complex life cycles known for living organisms. Following meiosis, four haploid tetraspores are produced, which germinate to produce either a male or a female gametophyte. When mature, the male gametophyte produces special spermatangial branches that bear structures, called spermatangia, which contain spermatia, the male gametes. The female gametophyte produces special carpogonial branches that bear carpogonia, the female gametes. Fertilization occurs when a male spermatium, carried by water currents, "bumps into" the extended portion of a female carpogonium and the two gametes fuse. The fertilized carpogonium (the zygote) and the female gametophyte tissue around it develop into a basket-like or pustule-like structure called a carposporophyte. The carposporophyte eventually produces and releases diploid carpospores that develop into tetrasporophytes. Certain cells of the tetrasporophyte undergo meiosis to produce tetraspores, and the cycle is repeated. In the life cycle of *Polysiphonia*, and many other red algae, there are separate male and female gametophytes, carposporophytes that develop on the female gametophytes, and separate tetrasporophytes.

The life cycles of diatoms, which are diploid, are also unique. Diatom walls, or frustules, are composed of two overlapping parts (the valves). During cell division, two new valves form in the middle of the cell and partition the protoplasm into two parts. Consequently, the new valves are generally somewhat smaller than the originals, so after many successive generations, most of the cells in the growing population are smaller than their parents. When such diatoms reach a critically small size, sexual reproduction may be stimulated. The small diploid cells undergo meiosis, and among pennate (thin, elliptical) diatoms the resulting haploid gametes fuse into a zygote, which grows quite large and forms a special kind of cell called an auxospore. The auxospore divides, forming two large, vegetative cells, and in this manner the larger size is renewed. In centric diatoms there is marked differentiation between nonmotile female gametes, which act as egg cells, and motile (typically uniflagellate) male gametes.

EVOLUTION AND PALEONTOLOGY

Modern ultrastructural and molecular studies have provided important information that has led to a reassessment of the evolution of algae. In addition, the fossil record for some groups of algae has hindered evolutionary studies, and the realization that some algae are more closely related to protozoa or fungi than they are to other algae came late, producing confusion in evolutionary thought and delays in understanding the evolution of the algae.

Ancient lineages of algae are believed to have given rise to a number of different organisms, ranging from green plants to protozoan euglenophytes. The latter are believed to have arisen from an ancient lineage of algae that included some zooflagellates, which is supported by ultrastructural and molecular data. Some scientists consider the colourless euglenophytes to be an older group and believe that the chloroplasts were incorporated by symbiogenesis more recently. The order of algae with the best fossil record are the Dasycladales, which are calcified unicellar forms of elegant construction dating back at least to the Triassic Period.

Some scientists consider the red algae, which bear little resemblance to any other group of organisms, to be very primitive eukaryotes that evolved from the prokaryotic blue-green algae (cyanobacteria). Evidence in support of this view includes the nearly identical photosynthetic pigments and the very similar starches among the red algae and the blue-green algae. Many scientists, however, attribute the similarity to an endosymbiotic origin of the red algal chloroplast from a blue-green algal symbiont.

Other scientists suggest that the red algae evolved from the cryptophytes (unicellular, aquatic algae), with the loss of flagella, or from fungi by obtaining a chloroplast. In support of this view are similarities in mitosis and in cell wall plugs, special structures inserted into holes in the cell walls that interconnect cells. Some evidence suggests that such plugs regulate the intercellular movement of solutes. Ribosomal gene sequence data from studies in molecular biology suggest that the red algae arose along with animal, fungal, and green plant lineages. The green algae are evolutionarily related, but their origins are unclear. The Prasinophyceae, which contains the genus *Micromonas*, is believed to be one of the most ancient groups of chlorophytes, and some fossil data support this view.

The photosynthetic algal dinoflagellates (dinophytes) are of uncertain origin. During the 1960s and '70s the unusual structure and chemical composition of the nuclear DNA of the dinophytes were interpreted as somewhat primitive features. Some scientists even considered these organisms to be mesokaryotes (intermediate between the prokaryotes and the eukaryotes); however, this view is no longer accepted. Their peculiar structure is considered as a result of evolutionary divergence, perhaps about 300 or 400 million years ago. The dinophytes may be distantly related to the chromophytes (chromists), but ribosomal gene sequence data suggest that their closest living relatives are the ciliated protozoa. It is likely that dinophytes arose from nonphotosynthetic ancestors and that later some species adopted chloroplasts by symbiogenesis and thereby became capable of photosynthesis, although many of these organisms still retain the ability to ingest solid food, similar to protozoa.

The origin of chromophytes also remains unknown. Ultrastructural and molecular data suggest that they are in a protistan lineage that diverged from the protozoa and aquatic fungi about 300 to 400 million years ago. At that time, chloroplasts were incorporated, originally as endosymbionts, and since then the many chromophyte groups have been evolving. Fossil, ultrastructural, and ribosomal gene sequence data support this hypothesis.

The cryptophytes are an evolutionary enigma. They have no fossil record, and phylogenetic data are conflicting. Although some workers align them near the red algae, because both groups possess phycobiliproteins in their chloroplasts, most scientists suggest that independent symbiotic origins for the red or blue colour of their chloroplasts could explain the similarity. Cryptophytes have flagellar hairs and other flagellar features that resemble those of the chromophyte algae. However, the mitochondrial structure and other ultrastructural features are distinct and argue against such a relationship.

The fossil record for the algae is not nearly as complete as it is for land plants and animals. Red algal fossils are the oldest known algal fossils. Microscopic spherical algae (*Eosphaera* and *Huroniospora*) that resemble the living genus *Porphyridium* are known from the Gunflint Iron Formation, a rock layer formed about 1.9 billion years ago in western Ontario, Canada. Fossils that resemble modern tetraspores are known from the Amelia Dolomites of Australia (formed some 1.5 billion years ago). The best characterized fossils are the coralline red algae represented in fossil beds since the Precambrian time.

Some of the green algal classes are also very old. Organic cysts resembling modern prasinophyte cysts date from about 1.2 billion years ago. *Tasmanites* formed the Permian "white coal," or tasmanite, deposits of Tasmania and accumulated to a depth of several feet in deposits that extend for miles. Similar deposits in Alaska yield up to 150 gallons of oil per ton of sediment. Certain ulvophyte (e.g., sea lettuce) fossils that date from about one billion years ago are abundant in Paleozoic rocks. Some green algae deposit calcium carbonate on their cell walls, and these algae produce extensive limestone formations. The charophytes (a group of green algae), as represented by the large stoneworts, date from about 400 million years ago. The oospore, the fertilized female egg, has spirals on its surface that were imprinted by the spiraling protective cells that surrounded the oospore. Oospores from before about 225 million years ago had right-handed spirals, whereas those formed since that time have had left-handed spirals. The reason for the switch remains a mystery.

Fossil dinophytes date from the Silurian Period (430 million years ago). Some workers consider at least a portion of the acritarchs, a group of cyst-like fossils of unknown affinity, to be dinophytes, but few scientists agree with that view. The acritarchs occurred as early as 700 million years ago.

The chromophytes have the shortest fossil history among the major algal groups. Some scientists believe that the group is ancient, whereas others point out that there is a lack of data to support this view and suggest that the group evolved recently, as indicated by fossil and molecular data. The oldest chromophyte fossils, putative brown algae, are approximately 400 million years old. Coccolithophores, coccolith-bearing haptophytes, date from the Late Triassic Epoch (230 to 200 million years ago), with one reported from approximately 280 million years ago. Coccolithophores were extremely abundant during the Mesozoic Era, contributing to deep deposits such as those that constitute the white cliffs of southeast England. Most species became extinct at the end of the Cretaceous Period (65.5 million years ago), along with the dinosaurs, and indeed there are more extinct species of coccolithophores than there are living species. The chrysophytes, bacillariophytes, and dictyochophytes (axodines; a group of heterokonts) date from about 100 million years ago, and despite the mass extinctions 65.5 million years ago, many species still flourish. In Lompoc, Calif., U.S., their siliceous remains have formed deposits of diatomite almost 0.5 km (0.3 mile) in depth, while at Mývatn in Iceland the lake bottom bears significant amounts of diatomite in the form of diatomaceous ooze, many metres in depth.

The xanthophytes may be even more recent, with fossils dating from about 20 million years ago, while fossil records of the remaining groups of algae, notably the euglenophytes and the cryptophytes, which lack mineralized walls, are negligible.

TYPES OF ALGAE

Although many algae are now placed in groups containing other types of protists that share a common ancestry (monophyletic arrangements), due to the absence of evolutionary information, other groups remain paraphyletic (containing members that descend from different, often unknown ancestors). One of the largest groups of algae is the heterokont algae (Heterokontophyta), which includes the chrysophytes (golden algae), the phaeophytes (brown algae), the xanthophytes (yellow algae), and the bacillariophytes (diatoms), as well as certain colourless algae. The rhodophytes (Rhodophyta; red algae) differ from other types of algae in that they are among the most ancient algae. As a result, they have their own phylum (or division). Likewise, the haptophytes (Haptophyta), which include the coccolithophores, and the chlorophytes (Chlorophyta), otherwise known as the green algae, are unique from all other algal forms, and hence each is given its own phylum (division) as well. Yet, despite these generally accepted groupings, many other algal protists await characterization and classification. As a consequence, the way in which certain algae are grouped today may change once more is known about their ancestries.

CLASSIFICATION FEATURES

Research using electron microscopes has demonstrated differences in features, such as the flagellar apparatus, cell division process, and organelle structure and function, that are important in the classification of algae. Similarities and differences among algal, fungal, and protozoan groups have led scientists to propose major taxonomic changes, and these changes are continuing. Molecular studies, especially comparative gene sequencing, have supported some of the changes that followed electron microscopic studies, but they have suggested additional changes as well. Furthermore, the apparent evolutionary scatter of some algae among protozoan and fungal groups implies that a natural classification of algae as a class is impracticable.

Kingdoms are the most encompassing of the taxonomic groups, and scientists are actively debating which organisms belong in which kingdoms. Some scientists have suggested as many as 30 or more kingdoms, while others have argued that all eukaryotes should be combined into one large kingdom. Using cladistic analysis (a method for determining evolutionary relationships), the green algae should be grouped with the land plants, the chromophyte-like algae should be grouped with the aquatic fungi and certain protozoa, and the euglenophyte-like algae are most closely related to the trypanosome flagellates, including the protozoa that cause sleeping sickness. However, it is unclear where the red algae or cryptomonads belong, and the overall conclusion is that the algae are not all closely related, and they do not form a single evolutionary lineage devoid of other organisms.

Division-level classification, as with kingdom level classification, is tenuous for algae. For example, in the past, some phycologists placed the classes Bacillariophyceae, Phaeophyceae, and Xanthophyceae in the division Chromophyta, whereas others placed each class in separate divisions: Bacillariophyta, Phaeophyta, and Xanthophyta. Today, the organisms forming these groups fall into the broad category of Heterokontophyta. Still, almost all phycologists agree on the definitions used to distinguish between the bacillariophytes, phaeophytes, and xanthophytes. In another example, the number of groups of green algae (Chlorophyta), and the algae placed in those groups, has varied greatly since 1960. Regardless of how the algae are divided taxonomically, their known structural and biochemical differences are useful for understanding their form and function in nature.

As a result, despite the confusion that plagues algae and protist classification, much can be learned from basic studies of the structure of flagellate cells (e.g., scales, angle of flagellar insertion, microtubular roots, and striated roots), the nuclear division process (mitosis), the cytoplasmic division process (cytokinesis), and the cell covering.

SELECT GROUPS OF ALGAE

Studying general groups of algae, such as the green algae, brown algae, and red algae, offers an opportunity to better understand the fundamental differences between these organisms. Their basic characteristics provide important information concerning not only their structure and biochemical properties but also their ecological and commercial significance. Within the larger groups of algae are many genera, and it is at this level—among organisms such as *Volvox*, kelp, and Irish moss—that the amazing diversity of algae becomes apparent.

GREEN ALGAE

Some 9,000 to 12,000 species of green algae (Chlorophyta) have been described. The photosynthetic pigments (chlorophylls *a* and *b*, carotene, and xan-

Caulerpa sertularioides is known familiarly as green feather alga.

thophyll) of green algae are in the same proportions as those in higher plants. The typical green algal cell, which can be motile or nonmotile, has a central vacuole, pigments contained in plastids that vary in shape in different species, and a two-layered cellulose and pectin cell wall. Food is stored as starch in pyrenoids (proteinaceous cores within the plastids). Green algae, variable in size and shape, include single-celled (*Chlamydomonas*, desmids), colonial (*Hydrodictyon*, *Volvox*), filamentous (*Spirogyra*, *Cladophora*), and tubular (*Actebularia*, *Caulerpa*) forms. Sexual reproduction is common, with gametes that have two or four flagella. Asexual reproduction is by cell division (*Protococcus*), motile or nonmotile spores (*Ulothrix*, *Oedogonium*), and fragmentation.

Most green algae occur in freshwater, usually attached to submerged rocks and wood or as scum on stagnant water. There are also terrestrial and marine species. Freefloating microscopic species serve as food and oxygen sources for aquatic organisms. Green algae are also important in the evolutionary study of plants. For example, the single-celled *Chlamydomonas* is considered similar to the ancestral form that probably gave rise to land plants.

Acetabularia

Acetabularia is a genus of one-celled, umbrella-like green algae found in subtropical seas. These organisms are commonly called the "mermaid's wine glass." At the top of the tall, slender stalk, 0.5 to 10 cm (0.2 to 3.9 inches) long, is a ring of branches that may be separate or fused to form a cap. Near the base of its stalk, *Acetabularia* has a large nucleus that divides many times when the alga matures and reproductive structures form. Streaming cytoplasm carries the daughter nuclei to the saclike sporangium of each umbrella lobe. Because part of one species can be grafted onto another, *Acetabularia* has been used to study the relative role of nucleus and cytoplasm in the genetic control of growth and development.

CHLAMYDOMONAS

Chlamydomonas is a genus of green biflagellated single-celled organisms. *Chlamydomonas* is considered a primitive life-form of evolutionary significance. The more or less oval cells have a cellulose membrane (theca), a stigma (eyespot), and a usually cup-shaped, pigment-containing chloroplast. Although photosynthesis occurs, nutrients also may be absorbed through the cell surface. Asexual reproduction is by zoospores, and sexual reproduction is by formation of gametes. The development of motility, sexual differentiation, and gamete fusion seems dependent on the production of substances (termones, gamones) that have a regulatory action similar to hormones.

There are some 500 species of *Chlamydomonas*, found in soil, ponds, and ditches, where they may colour water green. One species, *C. nivalis*, which contains the red pigment hematochrome, sometimes imparts a red colour to melting snow.

CHLORELLA

Chlorella is a genus of green algae found either singly or clustered in fresh or saltwater and in soil. The alga cellisspherical and has a cup-shaped chloroplast. *Chlorella*'s reproduction is asexual by non-motile reproductive cells (autospores). It has been extensively used in photosynthetic studies, in mass cultivation experiments, and for purifying sewage effluents. Because *Chlorella* multiplies rapidly and is rich in proteins and B-complex vitamins, it has also been studied as a potential food product for humans both on Earth and in outer space. *Chlorella* farms have been established in the United States, Japan, the Netherlands, Germany, and Israel. *Chlorella*'s effectiveness in sewage purification depends on its synthesis of a growth-inhibiting substance (chlorellin) that may suppress bacterial growth.

DESMIDS

Desmids are single-celled (sometimes filamentous or colonial), microscopic green algae that are characterized by extensive variation in cell shape. Typically the cell is divided symmetrically into semicells connected at a central isthmus. The three-layered cell wall is impregnated with openings or pores and pectin spicules. Irregular desmid movement is caused by the flow of a gelatinous substance through these pores. Conjugation (temporary union for the exchange of nuclear material) is the usual method of sexual generation. In some species a conjugation tube is formed. In others the two conjugant protoplasts unite in a gelatinous sheath that surrounds the cells. Usually cell division occurs in the region of the isthmus, each half develops another semicell, and in due course two complete desmids are formed. Spores are rare.

The distribution of desmids is worldwide, usually in acid bogs or lakes. Since most species have a limited ecological range, the presence of specific desmids is helpful in characterizing water samples. One of the more common desmid genera, the sickle-shaped *Closterium*, often contains gypsum crystals in cell vacuoles.

SPIROGYRA

Spirogyra is a genus of green algae found only in freshwater and usually free-floating. The slippery unbranched filaments are composed of cylindrical cells containing one or more beautiful spiral green chloroplasts, from which the genus gets its name. The nucleus is suspended in the central vacuole by fine cytoplasmic filaments. Vegetative reproduction is by fragmentation of the filaments. In sexual conjugation, cells of two strands lying side by side are joined by the outgrowths, or conjugation tubes, and the contents of one cell pass into and fuse with the contents of the other. The resulting fused cell (zygote) becomes surrounded by a thick wall and overwinters, while the vegetative filaments die.

On bright spring or fall days, there might be masses of *Spirogyra* floating near the surface of streams and ponds, buoyed by oxygen bubbles released during photosynthesis. During the night, when photosynthesis decreases, the masses tend to sink.

STONEWORT

Stoneworts are any of certain green algae of the class Charophyceae. Most stoneworts generally occur in freshwater. Some are calcified (*Chara*) and may accumulate as calcium carbonate deposits. These deposits may be so extensive that they form the major part of the calcareous marl of lakes and are sometimes a detrimental weed in fish hatcheries. Superficially resembling the structures of some higher plants, stonewort structures include rootlike rhizoids, whorls of branches at regular intervals, and an erect cylindrical axis, which may be surrounded by a sheath of small cells. In sexual reproduction each female sex organ (oogonium) contains one large egg, and each male sex organ (antheridium) produces one small, biflagellate sperm. An envelope of sterile cells surrounds the reproductive structures. No motile spores are formed. They are submerged and attached to the muddy bottoms of fresh or brackish rivers and lakes.

Volvox

Volvox is a genus of freshwater, chlorophyll-containing green algae. The spherical or oval hollow colonies, one cell in depth and sometimes exceeding the size of a pinhead, contain from 500 to 60,000 cells embedded in a gelatinous wall. Asexual colonies have biflagellated somatic cells and reproductive cells (gonidia) that produce small daughter colonies within the parent. Developing ova or spermatozoa replace gonidia in sexual colonies. Fertilization of eggs results in zygotes, which encyst and are released from the parent colony after its death. Thick-walled zygotes formed late in the summer serve as winter resting stages.

Volvox exhibits differentiation between somatic and reproductive cells, a phenomenon considered by some zoologists to be significant in tracing the evolution of higher animals from protozoans. Certain species, in which somatic cells appear to be joined by cytoplasmic strands, may be considered as multicellular organisms.

BROWN ALGAE

About 1,500 species of brown algae, or phaeophytes (Heterokontophyta), are known. These organisms are common in cold waters along continental coasts. Freshwater species are rare. Species colour varies from dark brown to olive green, depending upon the proportion of brown pigment (fucoxanthin) to green pigment (chlorophyll). Some brown seaweeds have gas-filled bladders (pneumatocysts), which keep photosynthetic parts of the algal thallus floating on or near the surface of the water. Brown algae vary in form and size from small filamentous epiphytes (*Ectocarpus*) to complex giant kelps that range in size from 1 metre to more than 100 metres (3.3 to 330 feet; *Laminaria, Macrocystis, Nerocystis*). Rockweed, another type of brown algae, is found attached to rocky coasts in temperate zones (*Fucus, Ascophyllum*) or floating freely (*Sargassum*). Brown algae multiply by asexual and sexual reproduction, and both the motile zoospores and gametes have two unequal flagella. Once a major source of iodine and potash, brown algae are still an important source of algin, a colloidal gel used as a stabilizer in the baking and ice-cream industries. Certain species are also

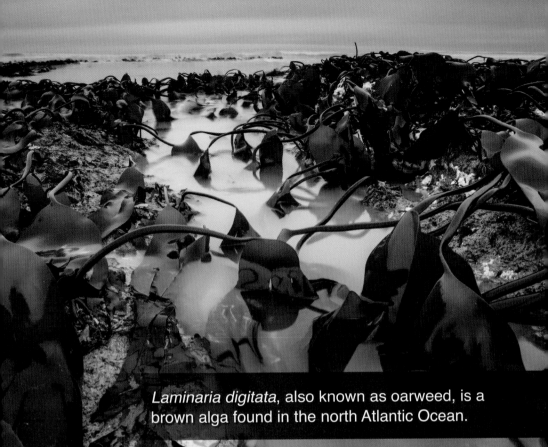

Laminaria digitata, also known as oarweed, is a brown alga found in the north Atlantic Ocean.

used as fertilizer, and several are eaten as a vegetable (e.g., *Laminaria*) in East Asia. Brown algae of the order Laminariales are popularly called kelps.

Diatoms

Diatoms, or bacillariophytes (Heterokontophyta), are algae found in sediments or attached to solid substances in freshwater and marine environments. About 16,000 species of diatoms have been described. They may be either unicellular or colonial. The silicified cell wall forms a pillbox-like shell (frustule) composed of

overlapping halves (epitheca and hypotheca) perforated by intricate and delicate patterns useful in
testing the resolving power of microscope lenses.

During reproduction, usually by cell division, the
overlapping shell halves separate, and each secretes
a (usually) smaller bottom half. Thus, individual diatoms formed from successive bottom halves show a
progressive decrease in size with each division. In a
few months there can be as much as a 60 percent
decrease in average size. Periodic spore formation
serves to restore the diatom line to its original size.

Food is stored as oil droplets, and the golden-
brown pigment fucoxanthin masks the chlorophyll
and carotenoid pigments that are also present. Diatoms, among the most important and prolific microscopic sea organisms, serve directly or indirectly as
food for many animals. Diatomaceous earth, a substance composed of fossil diatoms, is used in filters,
insulation, abrasives, paints, and varnishes and as a
base in dynamite.

FUCUS

Fucus (commonly known as rockweed) is a genus
of brown algae, the members of which are common
on rocky seacoasts and in salt marshes of northern temperate regions. Adaptations to its environment include bladder-like floats (pneumatocysts),
disk-shaped holdfasts for clinging to rocks, and

mucilage-covered blades that resist desiccation and temperature changes. *Fucus* is between about 2 and 50 cm (0.8 to 20 inches) in length, with growth of the thallus localized at the tips of forked shoots. The male and female reproductive organs may occur on the same or separate organisms, and some species produce eggs and sperm all year long. *Fucus* is a perennial alga with a lifespan of up to four years. *Fucus* species, along with kelp, are an important source of alginates—colloidal extracts with many industrial uses similar to those of agar.

Kelp

Kelp are large coastal seaweeds growing in colder seas and belonging to the order Laminariales of brown algae. Until early in the 19th century the ash of such seaweeds was an important source of potash and iodine. Giant kelps, of the genus *Macrocystis*, are rich in minerals and produce algin, a complex carbohydrate (polysaccharide) useful in various industrial processes, including tire manufacture. Algin is added to ice cream before freezing to prevent ice crystallization and is also used as a suspending and emulsifying agent in other food products.

Laminaria, a large brown seaweed (1 to 3 metres [3.3 to 9.8 feet] long) abundant along the Pacific and Atlantic coasts, has a stipe that superficially resembles the stem of land plants. Growth extension occurs at the meristematic region between the stipe (which is perennial) and the blade (which is shed annually).

Macrocystis, the largest known kelp, up to 65 metres (215 feet) long, is limited in distribution because it reproduces only at temperatures below 18–20 °C (64–68 °F). The complicated kelp body, in some ways similar in appearance to that of higher plants, has a large rootlike holdfast for attachment to the ocean floor, a stemlike stipe for the internal transport of organic material, and long branching stalks with blades that stay afloat by means of gas bladders.

Nereocystis, an annual kelp that grows primarily in deep waters and rapid tideways, can attain lengths up to 40 metres (130 feet). Internally the plant structure is similar to *Macrocystis*, and externally the stalk is tough and whiplike, terminating in a single large bladder containing up to 10 percent of carbon monoxide. The long leafy outgrowths from the stalk carry out photosynthesis and reproduction.

SARGASSUM

Sargassum (commonly called gulfweed) is a genus of brown algae (150 species), members of which are generally found attached to rocks along coasts in temperate regions. The Sargasso Sea is characterized by a free-floating mass of seaweed, predominately *S. natans* and *S. fluitans*, in the western Atlantic Ocean.

Sargassum is also known as sea holly because of its highly branched thallus with hollow, berry-like floats (pneumatocysts) and many leaflike sawtooth-edged blades. It is used as fertilizer in New Zealand. Most species reproduce sexually, but *S. natans* reproduces only by fragmentation.

Yellow-Green Algae

Yellow-green algae, or xanthophytes (Heterokontophyta), are distinguished by their food reserve (oil), the quantity of β-carotene in their plastids, and motile cells with unequal flagella. Frequently their cell walls are two overlapping halves. Approximately 600 species of yellow-green algae have been described.

The usual method of asexual reproduction in yellow green algae is by motile zoospores or nonmotile resting aplano spores. Sexual reproduction among these organisms is rare, although the genus *Vaucheria* is an important exception.

Vaucheria

Vaucheria is a genus of yellow-green algae with cells characterized by the presence of multinucleate tubular branches lacking cross walls except in association with reproductive organs or an injury. Food is stored as oil globules. Asexual reproduction is by motile multiflagellate zoospores and nonmotile aplanospores; sexual reproduction also occurs. The spherical female sex organ (oogonium) and the slender hookshaped male sex organ (antheridium) are usually produced on branches close to each other. After the nonmotile egg is fertilized by a biflagellate sperm, the zygote may enter a resting phase for several weeks before germinating into a new plant. Most species occur in freshwater, and some are marine.

DINOFLAGELLATES

Dinoflagellates are any of numerous one-celled aquatic organisms bearing two dissimilar flagellae and having characteristics of both plants and animals. Most are microscopic and marine. Dinoflagellates range in size from about 5 to 2,000 micrometres (0.0002 to 0.08 inch). Nutrition among dinoflagellates is plantlike, animallike, or mixed, and some species are parasitic or commensal. About one-half of the species are photosynthetic, but even among these many are also predatory. The group is an important component of phytoplankton in all but the colder seas and is an important link in the food chain. Dinoflagellates also produce some of the bioluminescence sometimes seen in the sea.

The dinoflagellate cell is banded by a median or coiled groove, the annulus, which contains a

Dinoflagellate blooms, which can be poisonous, can also create a bioluminescent glow over the water surface.

flagellum. A longitudinal groove, the sulcus, extends from the annulus posteriorly to the point at which a second flagellum is attached. The nuclei of dinoflagellates are larger than those of other eukaryotes. So-called armoured dinoflagellates are covered with cellulose plates, which may have long, spiny extensions. Some species lacking armour have a thin pellicle (protective layer). Photosynthetic dinoflagellates have yellowish or brownish plastids (pigment-containing bodies) and may store food in the form of starches, starch-like compounds, or oils.

Although sexual processes have been demonstrated in a few genera, reproduction is largely by binary or multiple fission. Under favourable conditions dinoflagellate populations may reach 60 million organisms per litre of water. Such dense growths, called blooms, can result in the red tides that discolour the sea and may poison fish and other marine animals. Some dinoflagellates produce toxins that are among the most poisonous known.

CERATIUM

Ceratium is a genus of single-celled aquatic algae common in freshwater and salt water from the Arctic to the tropics. Its members are armoured dinoflagellates. The cell contains chromatophores with yellow, brown, or green pigments. The theca, or armour, is composed of many textured plates that form one anterior horn and usually two posterior horns, which may help to slow the sinking of the cells. The spines tend to be shorter and thicker in cold, salty water and longer and thinner in less salty, warmer water. Members of the genus form an important part of the plankton found in temperate-zone seas.

GONYAULAX

Gonyaulax is a genus of dinoflagellates that inhabit fresh, saline, or brackish water. Members are covered by closely fitting cellulose plates and have two flagella: one extends backward from a longitudinal groove in the armour, and the other, in an encircling groove, may help to keep the animal afloat. There is no eyespot (stigma), and the pigment-containing chromatophores are yellow to dark brown. A species known as *G. catenella*, a toxic planktonic form, is sometimes abundant enough to colour water and cause the phenomenon called red tide, which

RED TIDE

Red tide is a discoloration of sea water that is usually caused by dinoflagellates during periodic blooms (or population increases). Toxic substances released by these organisms into the water may be lethal to fish and other marine life. Red tides occur worldwide in warm seas. Up to 50 million cells per litre (quart) of the species *Gymnodinium brevis* caused a red tide off the Florida coast in 1947 and turned the water from green to yellow to amber; thousands of fishes died. A red tide along the Northumberland coast in England in 1968 was the cause of the death of many sea birds. Similar red tides, caused by *Gonyaulax polyedra*, have occurred off the California and Portuguese coasts. Toxins released into the water are irritating to the human respiratory system; they may become public health problems at coastal resorts when breaking waves release the toxic substances into the air.

may kill many fish and other animals. Humans may be poisoned by eating mussels that have ingested large quantities of *G. catenella*.

GYMNODINIUM

Gymnodinium is a genus of marine or freshwater dinoflagellates. Members of the genus are bilaterally symmetrical with a delicate pellicle and disk-shaped chromatophores, which, when present, contain yellow, brown, green, or blue pigments. The genus is claimed by both botanists and zoologists, for, like all dinoflagellates, it has both plantlike and animallike species. Some species are photosynthetic; others require solid food. Some may be bioluminescent or form periodic blooms that may colour water yellow or red. A few species produce a toxin similar to that of the dinoflagellate *Gonyaulax*. Both toxins are fatal to fish and can irritate the nose and throat of human beings if inhaled.

ZOOXANTHELLA

Zooxanthella is a flagellate protozoan (or alga) with yellow or brown pigments contained in chromatophores that lives in other protozoa (foraminiferans and radiolarians) and in some invertebrates. In illuminated conditions, zooxanthellae use the carbon dioxide and waste materials of the host, supplying oxygen and food substances in return. They spend their resting stage in the host; at times they escape and become free-swimming, independent flagellates. Examples of zooxanthellae are *Cryptomonas* and *Chrysidella*.

RED ALGAE

Red algae, or rhodophytes (Rhodophyta), are predominantly marine algae that are often found attached to other shore plants. More than 6,000 different species of these organisms have been described. Their morphological range includes filamentous, branched, feathered, and sheetlike thalli. In most species, thin protoplasmic connections provide continuity between cells. Their usual red or blue colour is the result of a masking of chlorophyll by phycobilin pigments (phycoerythrin and phycocyanin).

The reproductive bodies of red algae are nonmotile. The female sex organ, called a carpogonium, consists of a uninucleate region that functions as the egg and a trichogyne, or projection, to which male gametes become attached. The nonmotile male gametes (spermatia) are produced singly in male sex organs, the spermatangia.

Some red algae are important food plants (e.g., laver, dulse). They may retain both their colour and gelatinous nature when cooked. Industrially, Irish moss (*Chondrus*) is used as a gelatin substitute in

Dulse is an edible red seaweed common in Iceland, Ireland, and other areas.

puddings, toothpaste, ice cream, and preserves. Some species of *Corallina* and its allies are important, along with animal corals, in forming coral reefs and islands. Agar, a gelatin-like substance prepared primarily from *Gracilaria* and *Gelidium* species, is important as a culture medium for bacteria and fungi.

DULSE

Dulse (*Palmaria palmata*) is a red seaweed found along both coasts of the North Atlantic. When fresh, it has the texture of thin rubber. Both the amount of branching and size (ranging from 12 to about 40 cm [5 to 16 inches]) vary. Growing on rocks, mollusks, or larger seaweeds, dulse attaches by means of disks or rhizoids. Dulse, fresh or dried, is eaten with fish and butter, boiled with milk and rye flour, or as a relish. The gelatinous substance contained in dulse is a thickening agent. The alga imparts a reddish colour to the food with which it is mixed.

IRISH MOSS

Irish moss (*Chondrus crispus*; also known as carrageen) is a species of red tufted seaweed with thin fronds from 5 to 25 cm (2 to 10 inches) long that grows abundantly along the rocky parts of the Atlantic coast of the British Isles, continental Europe, and North America. The plant is cartilaginous, varying in colour from a greenish yellow to a dark purple. When sun-dried and bleached it has a yellowish, translucent, hornlike aspect and consistency. The principal constituent of Irish moss is a gelatinous substance, carrageenan, which can be extracted by boiling. Carrageenan is used for curing leather and as an emulsifying and suspending agent in pharmaceuticals, food products, cosmetics, and shoe polishes. In North America it is harvested from shallow water by dredging with special rakes. In Europe it is usually obtained from broken fronds cast ashore.

LAVER

Laver (*nori* in Japanese) is any member of the genus *Porphyra*, a group of marine red algae. The thallus, a sheet of cells embedded in a thin gelatinous stratum, varies in colour from deep brown or red to pink. Sexual reproductive structures are borne at the margin. Laver grows near the high-water mark of the intertidal zone in both Northern and Southern hemispheres. It grows best in nitrogen-rich water, such as is found near sewage outlets. Laver is harvested, dried, and used as food in greater amounts than any other seaweed. A major food crop, it is cultivated on ropes in extensive inshore fields in East Asia. It is used as a soup base, as a flavouring for other food, and as a covering for rice-filled sushi. On the Welsh and Scottish coasts, it is sometimes grilled on toast (sloke) and is reported to have an oyster-like taste.

CONCLUSION

The many different kinds of fungi, protists, and algae illustrate the vast degree of diversity that exists among life on Earth, but this diversity has also challenged previous assumptions about the evolutionary history of these organisms and the classification of them in relation to plants and animals. As biologists continue to reexamine classification schemes, they are also learning much more about the complexity of these organisms. In fact, it is widely held that many thousands of species of these organisms still await discovery. Meanwhile, scientists are learning more about the role of fungi, protists, and algae in human disease. By investigating the distribution and life cycles of organisms such as *Aspergillus*, *Plasmodium*, and *Trypanosoma*, scientists have been able to more clearly identify mechanisms and patterns of infection. Such studies have also fueled the development of new drugs to treat diseases such as malaria and sleeping sickness. As more becomes known about the intricate biochemical and molecular processes that underlie the ability of these organisms to cause disease, it is expected that methods for disease prevention and control will improve.

GLOSSARY

adenosine triphosphate (ATP) A molecule that stores and then releases chemical energy from food molecules. ATP is found in the cells of all living things.

anaerobic Occuring in the absence of free oxygen.

autotrophs Organisms that synthesize their own food from inorganic compounds.

chloroplast A structure within a plant cell that contains two pigments, chlorophyll *a* and *b*, which absorb light energy and convert it to chemical energy, a process called photosynthesis.

chromosome A threadlike structure in the nucleus of eukaryotic cells consisting of tightly condensed DNA and protein that carries genes.

diploid Consisting of two sets of chromosomes, or double the haploid.

endoplasmic reticulum A system of connected membranes that helps to move proteins and lipids inside of a cell.

epiphytic Relating to plants that either grow on or are attached to another plant and have no attachment to the ground.

eukaryotic Describing cells in which the genetic material is enclosed within a nuclear membrane.

flagella Thin filaments that some cells use for movement.

genome The entire genetic code of a living thing.

haploid Consisting of a single set of chromosomes, or half the diploid.

haustoria A specialized fungal feature made up of tiny tubes or branches starting from a fungi's hyphae. These tubes penetrate and absorb moisture and nutrients from a host's tissue.

heterotrophs Organisms that require an organic source of carbon to survive, such as sugars, proteins, fats, or amino acids.

hyphae Branched, tubular filaments surrounded by a rigid cell wall that form a typical fungus's body.

meiosis Part of the process of sexual reproduction in which diploid (double) chromosomes are reduced to haploid (single) ones, which leads to the production of sex cells, including spores in plants and gametes in animals.

motile Capable of moving.

mycelium A mass of hyphae filaments that makes up the body of a fungus, and, when mature, produces spores.

nonmotile Not exhibiting or capable of movement.

obligate Biologically necessary.

organelles Structures surrounded with enclosed membranes that are contained in a cell's cytoplasm.

osmotrophy When creatures such as protists eat by taking in dissolved nutrients from the medium in which they live.

phagotrophy When creatures such as protists eat by engulfing particulate food.

prokaryotic Describing cells in which the genetic material is not enclosed in a nuclear membrane.

protoplasm The cytoplasm and nucleus of a cell.

saprotroph An organism that feeds on nonliving organic matter.

spore A reproductive cell of a fungus.

sporophore The spore-produced part of a fungus.

vector An organism that can serve as a carrier of genetic material, such as a segment of DNA from a parasite, to another host.

BIBLIOGRAPHY

FUNGI AND LICHENS

Books for the general reader about the world of fungi include Nicholas P. Money, *The Triumph of the Fungi: A Rotten History* (2007); Brian M. Spooner and Peter Roberts, *Fungi* (2005); Roy Watling, *Fungi* (2003); Nicholas P. Money, *Mr. Bloomfield's Orchard: The Mysterious World of Mushrooms, Molds, and Mycologists* (2002); and David Moore, *Slayers, Saviours, Servants, and Sex: An Exposé of Kingdom Fungi* (2001). John Webster and Roland Weber, *Introduction to Fungi*, 3rd ed. (2007); Sarah C. Watkinson, Lynne Boddy, Nicholas P. Money, and Michael J. Carlile, *The Fungi*, 3rd ed. (2016); Bryce Kendrick, *The Fifth Kingdom*, 4th ed. (2017); and Kevin Kavanagh, *Fungi: Biology and Applications*, 2nd ed. (2011) are good introductions to the fungi.

Paul M. Kirk et al., Ainsworth & Bisby's *Dictionary of the Fungi*, 10th ed. (2008), remains the standard reference for terminology and definitions. David Moore and LilyAnn Novak Frazer, *Essential Fungal Genetics* (2002); Nick Talbot, *Molecular and Cellular Biology of Filamentous Fungi: A Practical Approach* (2001); and Dilip K. Arora and Randy M. Berka, *Applied Mycology and Biotechnology: Volume 5, Genes and Genomics* (2005), explore the genetics

and cellular biology of fungi. Discussions of physi-
ological topics of fungi include D.H. Jennings, The
Physiology of Fungal Nutrition (2007); and David H.
Griffin, *Fungal Physiology*, 2nd ed. (1996).

Thomas H. Nash, *Lichen Biology*, 2nd ed.
(2008); William Purvis, Lichens (2000); and James
N. Corbridge and William A. Weber, *Rocky Moun-
tain Lichen Primer* (1998), provide an introduction to
lichens. Irwin M. Brodo, Sylvia Duran Sharnoff, and
Stephen Sharnoff, *Lichens of North America* (2001);
and Margalith Galun, *CRC Handbook of Lichenology*,
vol. 2 (1988), are comprehensive works on lichenology and useful reference sources.

PROTISTS

Information on protists is presented in W. Foissner
and David L. Hawksworth (eds.), *Protist Diversity
and Geographical Distribution* (2009); and R. Weth-
erbee, R.A. Andersen, and J.D. Pickett-Heaps,
The Protistan Cell Surface (1994). Explorations of
the place of protists in the evolution of eukaryotes
include Laura A. Katz and Debashish Bhattacharya
(eds.), *Genomics and Evolution of Microbial Eukaryotes* (2006); and Wolfgang Loffelhardt (ed.), *Endosymbiosis* (2013).

ALGAE

Works that provide an introduction to algae include F.E. Round, *The Ecology of Algae* (1981); Christopher S. Lobban and Paul J. Harrison, *Seaweed Ecology and Physiology* (1994); Catriona L. Hurd et al., *Seaweed Ecology and Physiology*, 2nd ed. (2014); Robert Edward Lee, *Phycology*, 4th ed. (2008); Linda E. Graham and Lee Warren Wilcox, *Algae*, 2nd ed. (2009); Laura Barsanti and Paolo Gualtieri, *Algae: Anatomy, Biochemistry, and Biotechnology*, 2nd ed. (2014); and Colin S. Reynolds, *The Ecology of Phytoplankton* (2006).

Various groups of algae are studied in greater detail in J.C. Green, B.S.C. Leadbeater, and W.L. Diver (eds.), *The Chromophyte Algae: Problems and Perspectives* (1989); Carmelo R. Tomas and Grethe R. Hasle (eds.), *Identifying Marine Phytoplankton* (1997); F.E. Round, R.M. Crawford, and D.G. Mann, *The Diatoms: Biology and Morphology of the Genera* (1990, reissued 2007); Hilda Canter-Lund and John W.G. Lund, *Freshwater Algae: Their Microscopic World Explored* (1995); B.S.C. Leadbeater and J.C. Green (eds.), *The Flagellates: Unity, Diversity, and Evolution* (2000); John D. Wehr and Robert G. Sheath (eds.), *Freshwater Algae of North America: Ecology and Classification*, 2nd ed. (2015); Terumitsu Hori, *An Illustrated Atlas of the Life History of Algae*,

3 vol. (1994); Edna Granéli and Jefferson T. Turner (eds.), *Ecology of Harmful Algae* (2006); and Joseph Seckbach (ed.), *Algae and Cyanobacteria in Extreme Environments* (2007).

Analyses of the genetics and evolution of algae are found in Juliet Brodie and Jane Lewis (eds.), *Unravelling the Algae: The Past, Present, and Future of Algae Systematics (*2007); and Feng Chen and Yue Jiang (eds.), *Algae and Their Biotechnological Potential* (2001).

INDEX

A

Acetabularia, characteristics of, 224–225

Agaricales, types of, 92–94, 97

algae
  characteristics, 179–182, 219–220
  classification, 220–223
  commercial value, 187–193
  development of, 212–218
  environmental significance, 186
  habitat, 184–185
  size, 182–184
  structure and function, 196–212
  toxicity, 193–196
  types of, 222–245

Allomyces, 67, 68

"altruistic" vaccine, 169

Amanita, types of, 94–95

amoebas, characteristics of, 151–153

"antidisease" vaccine, 169

Armillaria, types of, 95–97

Ascomycota (sac fungi), types of, 76–90

asexual reproduction, types of, 62–64, 70

Aspergillus, types of, 82

Assembling the Fungal Tree of Life (AFTOL) project, 75

Auricularia auricula-judae (ear fungus), characteristics of, 91–92

B

Basidiomycota, types of, 90–100

beard lichen, characteristics of, 105, 107

bed nets, efficacy for preventing malaria, 169

Boletales, types of, 98–100

brown algae, characteristics of, 230–231

C

Ceratium, characteristics of, 238

Chagas' disease, 176

Chain, Ernst Boris, 17, 19, 83

Chlamydomonas, characteristics of, 225–226

Chlorella, characteristics of, 226

Chytridiomycota, 100

ciguatera disease, 194

ciliates, characteristics of, 153–155

Claviceps purpurea (ergot), 16, 19, 79

Cordyceps, 77, 79

Cryphonectria parasitica (chestnut blight), 77, 78–79

cup fungi, types of, 79–81

D

de Bary, Heinrich Anton, 71

desmids, characteristics of, 226–227

destroying angels, 95

diatoms, characteristics of, 231–232

dinoflagellates, characteristics of, 236–238

dulse, characteristics of, 243

E

edible fungi and lichens, 80–81, 107

Euglena, characteristics of, 155–156

Eurotiomycetes, types of, 81–82

F

finfish poisoning, 194

Five Kingdoms, 116

flagellates, characteristics of, 156–157

Fleming, Alexander, 16, 17, 19, 83

Florey, Howard Walter, 17, 19, 83

foraminiferan, 157–158

Fucus, characteristics of, 232–233

fungi
ecology, 70, 72
growth, 29–34
importance of, 15–17, 19–20
life cycles, 68–70, 71
reproductive processes, 62–68
size and range, 20–22
structure, 22–27, 29
sustenance, 34–38, 40–43, 45–48

G

Gonyaulax, characteristics of, 238–240

green algae, characteristics of, 222, 224–230

gregarines, characteristics of, 158–159

Gymnodinium, characteristics of, 240

H

Haeckel, Ernst, 110

Handbook of Protoctista, 117

helioflagellates, characteristics of, 159–160

heliozoans, characteristics of, 160

Helvela gigas (snow mushroom), 81

heterothallic fungi, 66–67

homothallic fungi, 67

honeybees, dysentery in, 104

humans, as nutrition for parasitic fungi, 42–43, 45–47

I

Iceland moss, characteristics of, 107

Irish moss, characteristics of, 243–244

Irish potato famines, 102, 103

K

kelp, characteristics of, 233–234

L

laver, characteristics of, 244–245

Leishmania, characteristics of, 161–162

lichens
form and function, 53–60
structure of, 14, 48–53
types of, 105, 107–109

live oak, blight and, 78

long-lasting insecticide-treated nets (LLINs), 169–170

Lycoperdaceae, types of, 97–98

lysergic acid diethylamide (LSD), 19

M

malaria, treatment and eradication of, 168–170

Margulis, Lynn, 110, 112, 115–117

meiosis, 64, 65, 68, 70, 142, 209, 210, 211, 212

Microsporidia, types of, 101–102
morels, 80–81
Mosquirix vaccine, 168
myxomycetes, characterstics of, 162–163

N

Neocallimastigomycota, 74
Neurospora (red bread mold), 16, 77
Nobel Prize, 17, 19
nosema disease, 104

O

oak moss, characteristics of, 107–108
one-gene-one-enzyme theory, 16
Oomycota, types of, 102–104
opalinids, characteristics of, 163–164
Origin of Eukaryotic Cells, 115

P

Paramecium, characteristics of, 164–166
parasexuality, 70
Parmelia, types of, 108–109

penicillin, discovery of, 16, 17, 19, 83
Penicillium, types of, 82–85
Penicililum notatum, 16, 17, 83
perfume, moss used in, 107–108
PfSPZ vaccine, 169
pheromones, 67
Phytophthora infestans (late blight), 102–104
plants, as nutrition for parasitic fungi, 37–38, 40–42
Plasmodium, characteristics of, 167, 170–171
plasmogamy, 68
Polyporales, types of, 99–100
post oak, blight and, 78
predatory fungi, 47–48
protists
    characteristics, 110–117
    development of, 139–144
    habitat, 133–139
    movement, 118–124
    reproduction and life cycles, 127–132
    respiration and nutrition, 124–127
    structure and function of, 117–118

Prototheca, 195
protozoans
    characteristics, 145–148
    classification, 148–151

R

radiolarians, characteristics
    of, 171–172
red algae, characteristics of,
    241, 243
red tides, 137, 185, 194, 238,
    239, 240
RTS,S malaria vaccine, 168

S

Saccharomyces cerevisiae
    (brewer's yeast), 15,
    77, 88–89
saprobiosis, 35–37
Sargassum, characteristics
    of, 234–235
saxitoxin, 193
Schwartz, Karlene, 116
serial endosymbiotic theory
    (SET), development of,
    115–117
sexual incompatibility, 66–67
sexual reproduction, descrip-
    tion of process in
    fungi, 64–66

shellfish poisoning, 193–194,
    195, 240
sirenin, 67
sleeping sickness, 176
slime mold, characteristics of,
    172–174
Sordariomycetes, types of, 85
Spanish chestnut, blight and,
    78
Spirogyra, characteristics of,
    227–228
spores, structure of, 27, 29
sporophores, structure of, 27,
    29
stentor, characteristics of,
    174–175
stoneworts, characteristics of,
    228–229
symbiosis, origin of term, 71
Symbiosis in Cell Evolution, 115

T

thallus, structure of, 23–27
Trebouxia, 53, 54
trichomonads, characteristics
    of, 175
trisporic acid, 68
truffles, types of, 85–88
trypanosomes, characteristics
    of, 176
tsetse flies, 176

U

Untersuchungen über die Brandpilze ("Researches Concerning Fungal Blights"), 71

V

Vaucheria, characteristics of, 235–236
Volvox, characteristics of, 229–230
vorticellas, characteristics of, 176–177

W

Whittaker, R.H., 110, 112, 114

Y

yeast, types of, 88–90
yellow-green algae, characteristics of, 235

Z

zooflagellates, characteristics of, 177–178
zooxanthella, characteristics of, 240–241